# ALTERNATIVE ANSWERS TO

# BACK

## PROBLEMS

# ALTERNATIVE ANSWERS TO

# BACK

## PROBLEMS

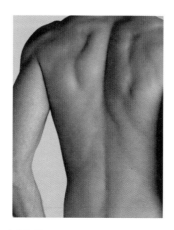

NIGEL HOWARD
CONSULTANT: DR LOÏC BURN

Grange
BOOKS

A QUANTUM BOOK

Published by Grange Books
an imprint of Grange Books Plc
The Grange
Kingsnorth Industrial Estate
Hoo, nr, Rochester
Kent ME3 9ND
www.grangebooks.co.uk

ISBN-10: 1-84013-933-1
ISBN-13: 978-1-84013-933-4

This book was produced by
Quantum Publishing Ltd
6 Blundell Street
London N7 9BH

QUM530

Printed in Singapore by
Star Standard Industries (Pte) Ltd

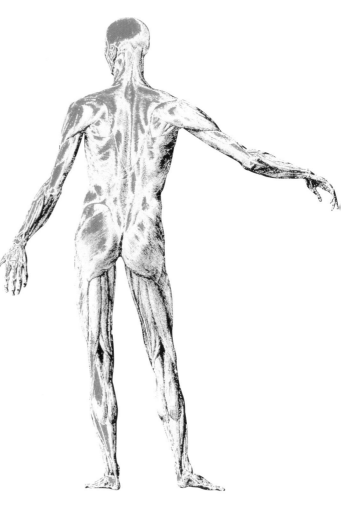

| | |
|---|---|
| EDITORS | Richard Shaw |
| | John C. Miles |
| DESIGNER | Sue Storey |
| ART EDITOR | Frances de Rees |
| COPY EDITOR | Lindsay McTeague |
| MANAGING EDITOR | Anne Yelland |
| MANAGING ART EDITOR | Patrick Carpenter |
| EDITORIAL DIRECTOR | Ellen Dupont |
| ART DIRECTOR | Sean Keogh |
| PICTURE RESEARCH | Zilda Tandy |
| | Elaine Willis |
| EDITORIAL COORDINATOR | Becca Clunes |
| EDITORIAL ASSISTANT | Sophie Sandy |
| INDEX | Laura Hicks |
| PRODUCTION | Nikki Ingram |
| DTP EDITOR | Lesley Gilbert |
| COVER PHOTOGRAPH | Tony Latham |

# Contents

# Introduction

In the nations of the industrialized West, back pain is increasing at an alarming rate. The reason for this rise in serious, disabling back pain is not clear, although many experts blame our increasingly sedentary lifestyle, both at work and at home. They point out that the populations of most Western nations are, on average, becoming older, fatter and less active – all important risk factors for back pain in their own right.

Back pain is a symptom, not a disease. It can have any number of different causes, some very minor in comparison with the resulting pain and disability, others complex and deep-rooted. In addition, back pain can be a symptom of illnesses and physical disorders that have nothing to do with the back. Family doctors, their clinics already overflowing, may have neither the time nor the specialized training to deal with cases that can be difficult and time-consuming to diagnose and even more difficult to treat. In the light of this, a growing number of people suffering from chronic conditions, such as back pain, skin complaints and allergies, are seeking and finding relief through alternative therapies.

The medical establishment is beginning to acknowledge the benefits of some therapies, especially osteopathy, chiropractic and acupuncture. Indeed, so effective are osteopathy and chiropractic as therapies for back pain that they are now considered almost "conventional" treatments.

The aim of this book is to give you an insight into your back, how it works, what can go wrong and how it can be treated. The fact that more space is devoted to "alternative" than to "conventional" medicine does not imply a value judgement, it is merely that there are more alternative therapies with reported benefits for back pain than conventional ones. In fact, many of these therapies have become so widespread and well regarded that even the description "alternative" is falling out of favour. The term "complementary therapies" is often preferred, to help emphasize that the so-called natural therapies should be viewed as complementary to conventional medical treatment rather than as alternatives to it.

The majority of episodes of back pain clear up by themselves within a few days. If not, you may consult your family doctor and have a perfectly satisfactory outcome. However, if your back pain does not get better or keeps recurring and your family doctor or hospital specialist cannot help, don't despair. Out there somewhere is the perfect therapy or combination of therapies for you.

Complementary practitioners have the time and training to look beyond the straightforward "scientific" approach of cause and effect and, instead, take a more holistic approach, viewing your symptoms in the context of your environment, personality and even emotional make-up. As a result, similar symptoms are often treated in completely different ways. Practitioners of Traditional Chinese Medicine have a saying that sums this up: "One disease, different treatments. Different diseases, one treatment."

Nigel Howard

# How to use this book

This book works in several ways. You can read from beginning to end to build up a picture of your back, how to avoid problems, what can go wrong and your treatment options. But you can also browse through it, using the "Find out more" suggestions as your guide, to learn all about a specific condition and its treatment. Or you could dip into the treatments and therapies chapter to explore all your options in overcoming a back problem, or learning to live with it.

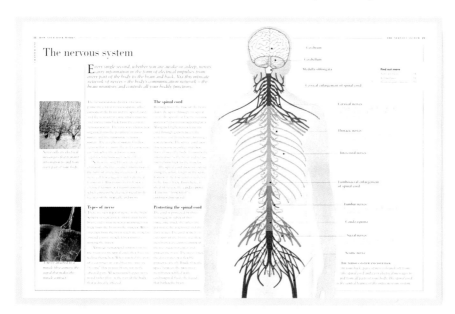

1 *Chapter One, How Your Back Works, looks at the bones, muscles and nerves in the three main systems involved in the functioning of the back. It explains the make-up of these systems and how they work and interact with each other.*

2 *Chapter Two, Treating Your Back Well, looks at how your back is used in daily life. Individual sections give detailed advice on posture and about how to protect your back from injury while bending, lifting and carrying. Special features cover topics including housework, choosing a bed, driving and travel. Handy checklists give advice on posture during different activities.*

3 *Chapter Three, Assessing Back Problems, deals with the things that can go wrong with your back and looks at skeletal, muscular and nerve problems, as well as referred pain and sports injuries. It includes a comprehensive list of sports and their suitability for back-pain sufferers. The chapter ends with an easy-to-read guide to your problem, its likely origin and its possible solution.*

4 *Chapter Four, Your Treatment Options, deals with the therapies themselves. It is divided into four sections: self-administered complementary therapies, practitioner-administered complementary therapies, conventional therapies and surgery. The chapter contains advice on choosing the right therapy for you and on finding a reliable practitioner.*

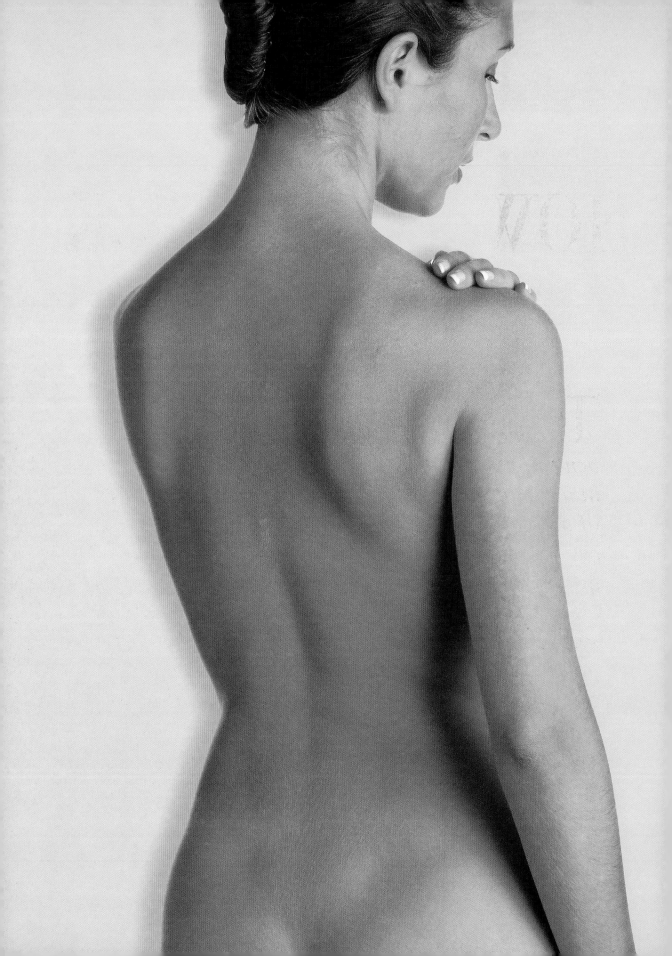

# 1

# HOW YOUR BACK

# WORKS

The human back is an engineering wonder. It allows you to walk upright, to balance, bend, twist, lift, jump and run. But all these movements depend upon the smooth functioning of a great many elements. Enormous demands are made upon the spine – it needs to be strong as well as flexible.

For the back to play its vital role, three distinct systems must work together – bones, muscles and nerves. Damage to a part of any of these systems can result in pain and disabling stiffness.

This chapter explores each of the three body systems and the ways in which they work together in the spine, the most important part of the body's structure.

# The skeletal system

*The skeleton is the bony structure that supports and protects the soft parts of your body. The skull encloses the brain; the rib cage shields vital internal organs; the pelvis holds the reproductive organs and intestines; the spinal column protects the spinal cord and is the central support for the whole body.*

**SKELETON**
*The spine is the central structure around which the skull, limbs and rib cage are all articulated.*

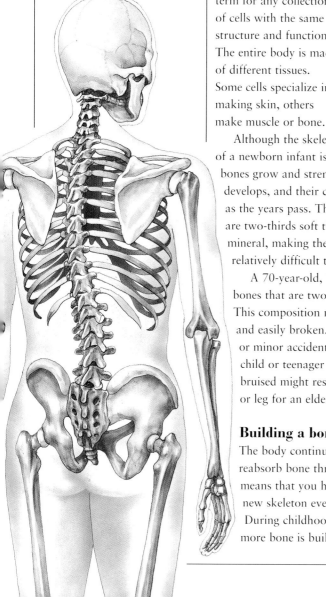

Bones are made of a mixture of soft tissue and calcium apatite, a hard, crystal-like mineral. "Tissue" is the medical term for any collection of cells with the same structure and function. The entire body is made of different tissues. Some cells specialize in making skin, others make muscle or bone.

Although the skeleton of a newborn infant is fully formed, the bones grow and strengthen as the child develops, and their consistency changes as the years pass. The bones of a child are two-thirds soft tissue and one-third mineral, making them flexible and relatively difficult to break.

A 70-year-old, by contrast, has bones that are two-thirds mineral. This composition makes them brittle and easily broken. This is why a fall or minor accident that would leave a child or teenager just shaken and bruised might result in a broken hip or leg for an elderly person with.

## Building a bone
The body continues to build and reabsorb bone throughout life, which means that you have a completely new skeleton every 20 years or so. During childhood and adolescence, more bone is built than is absorbed,

*Your spine is very flexible, allowing you to bend forward, backward and to both sides, and permits a huge range of everyday movements.*

and in most of adult life bone mass remains constant. But in old age the body absorbs more bone than it builds and this can lead to thinning of the bones, a condition known as osteoporosis. This can result in fractures or, in severe cases, the crumbling of bones.

## A curvy structure
Although there is a tendency to think of the spinal column as straight – people commonly tell children to "sit up straight" or describe someone as "straight-backed" – this is not the case. The spinal column actually consists of four gentle curves.

Starting from the top and working downward, the 7 cervical (neck) vertebrae curve slightly forward; the 12 thoracic (chest) vertebrae, to which the ribs are attached, curve backward to make space for the chest; the 5 lumbar (lower back) vertebrae curve forward again, producing the hollow in the small of the back; and the sacrum and coccyx curve backward. This structure makes the spinal column more flexible and better able to absorb the shocks, knocks, stresses and strains inflicted on it on a daily basis.

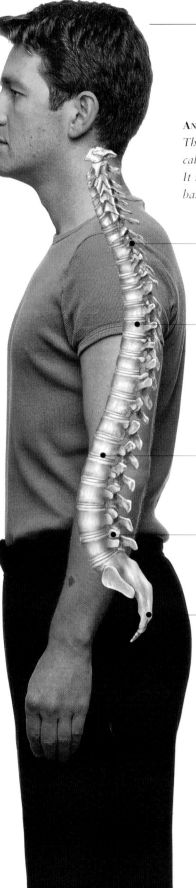

### ANATOMY OF THE SPINE

*The spinal column is made up of blocklike bones called vertebrae stacked on top of each another. It runs from the base of the skull to the pelvis, the basin-shaped bone that connects it to the legs.*

**Find out more**

| | |
|---|---|
| Muscular system | 16 |
| Skeletal problems | 40 |

### Cervical curvature
Seven vertebrae; together these allow movement of the head and neck.

### Thoracic curvature
Twelve vertebrae; these allow twisting movement of the trunk. Ribs attach to these vertebrae at points known as costal facets.

### Lumbar curvature
Five vertebrae; these allow bending and twisting movements.

### Sacral curvature
Five fused vertebrae; these support the spine and attach to the pelvis.

### Coccyx
Four fused vertebrae; they are a vestigial tail.

## Spine fact file

• A well as curving, the spine also tapers, with the smallest vertebra situated at the base of the skull and the largest attached to the pelvis.

• The length of the spine averages 70 cm (28 in) in men and 60 cm (24 in) in women.

• At birth, the spinal column consists of 33 separate bones, but by adulthood the bottom four, the coccygeal vertebrae, have joined together to form the coccyx, a tiny vestigial tail.

• The five bones above the coccyx, the sacral vertebrae, fuse to form the rear part of the pelvis, known as the sacrum.

## PARTS OF A TYPICAL VERTEBRA

*Each vertebra has a solid, weight-bearing section and a hole formed by the vertebral arch, which protects the spinal cord. Projecting bony or transverse processes make contact with those of the vertebrae above and below, and provide anchoring points for the various muscles and ligaments in the back.*

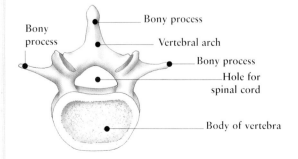

Bony process
Vertebral arch
Bony process
Hole for spinal cord
Bony process
Body of vertebra

# Joints, ligaments and discs

All vertebrae are of similar design, but they are not identical in size or shape. These differences govern the amount and direction of movement they can make when linked together by joints, supported by ligaments and cushioned by discs.

*Your body weight puts the spine under pressure, even when you are doing nothing more than simple walking. Being overweight exacerbates the stress on your spine.*

Without a supporting structure of joints, ligaments and discs, the vertebrae of the spine would rub together, causing pain.

## Joints

Facet joints occur where the processes of one vertebra fit against the processes of another. Here, as in other joints in the body, the bones are covered with a smooth layer of cartilage, a strong, elastic tissue that is extremely slippery – more slippery than ice. This prevents the friction that would result if the bones simply rubbed together. The cartilage-covered bones are sealed in a tough, fibrous joint capsule. The lining of the capsule secretes an oily fluid, synovial fluid, which lubricates the joint and helps it to move freely. The more you work, or move, a joint, the more synovial fluid will be secreted.

Altogether there are 149 joints in the spine. There are joints that connect the vertebrae to each other, as well as those that link the spine to other parts of the skeletal system. These include a joint between the first cervical vertebra and the base of the skull, joints attaching the ribs to processes at the back of the thoracic vertebrae and two joints at the bottom of the spine, the sacroiliac joints, where the sacrum joins the hip bones.

## Ligaments

Throughout the body, joints are supported and strengthened by ligaments, strong bands of tough fibrous tissue. Ligaments are not elastic but they do have some give. Their length determines the range of movement in any particular

*Running transmits shocks up the legs and pelvis to the spine. When your back is in good condition, these shocks are cushioned by the discs located between your vertebrae.*

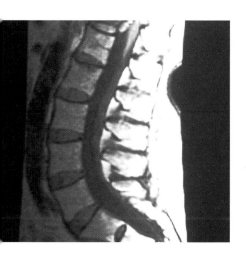

## DISCS AND VERTEBRAE

*A colour-enhanced X-ray of the human spine shows the discs, and vertebrae, of the lower back. Each disc is firmly attached to the vertebra above and below and acts as a joint as well as a shock absorber, allowing the spine to be both flexible and strong.*

*Carrying heavy bags of shopping squeezes the intervertebral discs, absorbing the stress of the load.*

joint, as ligaments stop joints from moving too far. In the back, the main ligaments run the whole length of the spine, up and down the front, back and sides, and help to keep it in one piece. In the facet joints, the ligaments are part of the joint capsule and hold the bones firmly together, preventing any slippage. Other ligaments connect the bones of the spine to the bones of the ribs and pelvis.

## Discs

When you walk, run or carry heavy bags of shopping your spine is subjected to a continuous series of shocks and stresses. To deal with this the spine has its own built-in shock absorbers.

Between the main body of each vertebra and its neighbour above and below is a tough but springy pad – the intervertebral disc. There are 23 of these discs in the human spine. Inside each disc's strong fibrous casing, the *annulus fibrosus*, there is a thick, gel-like substance, the *nucleus pulposus*. This means that a disc can be squeezed to cushion the stresses and strains of everyday life and then return to its original shape.

## Losing fluid

During the day the discs in your back gradually become compressed – some of the fluid part of the *nucleus pulposus* is squeezed out and absorbed by the vertebrae on either side. As you rest in bed at night, the discs reabsorb the fluid. This means that people are taller when they get out of bed in the morning and actually become shorter – about 2 cm (¾ in) on average – during the course of the day. In old age, however, the discs gradually dry out and become thinner. This has the effect of making old people shorter than they once were.

## DISC COMPRESSION

*The compressible nature of your intervertebral discs allows them to deform as you carry a load and then spring back into shape.*

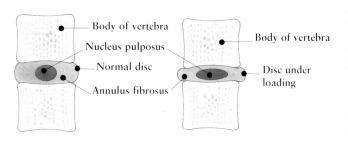

Body of vertebra
Nucleus pulposus
Normal disc
Annulus fibrosus

Body of vertebra
Disc under loading

# The muscular system

*W*hile your bones support you, it is your muscles that allow you to move. Muscles are bunches or bundles of long, thin fibres that are able to contract, or make themselves shorter, when told to do so by the nerves.

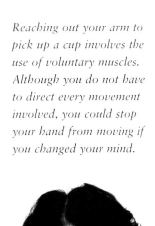

*Reaching out your arm to pick up a cup involves the use of voluntary muscles. Although you do not have to direct every movement involved, you could stop your hand from moving if you changed your mind.*

There are two main types of muscle in the body, involuntary and voluntary. Involuntary muscles operate without your conscious control, for example the muscles of the heart and the muscles that allow you to breathe. You do not have to tell your heart to beat or your lungs to expand and contract, it happens automatically.

Voluntary muscles, by contrast, are normally under your control, even if you do not consciously have to think about every single movement. If, for example, you decide to pick up a cup, your arm moves out and your hand grasps the cup and lifts it to your lips. You don't have to think about each individual part of the process, you just do it. The same thing happens when you decide to sit up, lie down, turn your head, look up or down or walk and run. It is usually enough to give your body a general instruction, which it then carries out in a series of reflex actions without your having to oversee each individual movement.

There are bunches of voluntary muscles around every joint in the body, either attached directly to the bones or to strips of tough tissue known as tendons. As a rule, these muscles work in pairs to move the bone in the joint – one contracts as the other relaxes.

## Reflex actions

Your voluntary muscles can also react in a reflex way if you are under threat or in danger.

Touching a hot stove causes you to snatch your hand away faster than you could consciously think to do it.

If you start to step on a tack or drawing pin, you react just as quickly to move your foot away from the sharp point.

## Muscles and your back

In the back, there are several layers of muscles that vary in size and function. In the deepest layer there are short, thick muscles extending from one vertebra to the next and sometimes covering several vertebrae. These muscles work to keep the bones of the spine in alignment and to control posture.

On top of this layer are long straplike muscles, most of which are attached to the rear of the pelvis and fan out as they travel up toward the head. They are attached to the ribs and vertebrae. These are the key back muscles involved in bending and straightening up again.

The largest muscles in the back are situated in the top layer. In the upper back, they run in triangular sheets across each side of the back and attach the vertebrae to the bones of the shoulders. In the lower back, these muscles connect the vertebrae to the hips.

## Muscles at the front

Stomach muscles play an important role in helping your back muscles to support and move the spine. They pull the rib cage closer to the pelvis, helping the spine to bend. In addition, the force they exert down the front of the body balances the

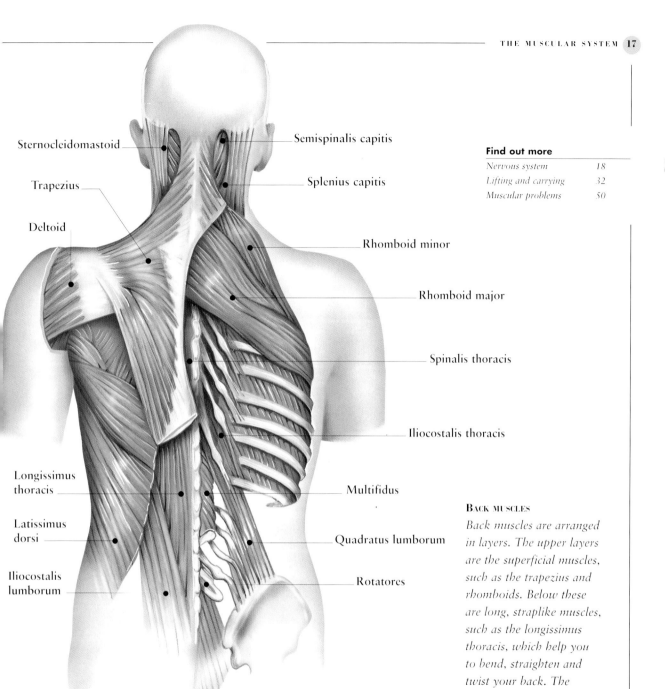

Sternocleidomastoid

Semispinalis capitis

Trapezius

Splenius capitis

Deltoid

Rhomboid minor

Rhomboid major

Spinalis thoracis

Iliocostalis thoracis

Longissimus
thoracis

Multifidus

Latissimus
dorsi

Quadratus lumborum

Iliocostalis
lumborum

Rotatores

**BACK MUSCLES**
*Back muscles are arranged in layers. The upper layers are the superficial muscles, such as the trapezius and rhomboids. Below these are long, straplike muscles, such as the longissimus thoracis, which help you to bend, straighten and twist your back. The deepest muscles, including the spinalis and rotatores groups, help to keep the spine in alignment.*

opposite pull from the back muscles. The muscles of your stomach also work with your back muscles to twist the trunk and control your posture when you lean backward or sideways.

When you lift heavy weights, stomach muscles also come into play. As you lift, both your stomach and back muscles tighten. This raises the pressure inside the abdominal cavity which, like an inflated balloon, is then capable of supporting weight. This takes stress off the spine and makes it easier for the back muscles to pull you into an upright position.

# The nervous system

*Every single second, whether you are awake or asleep, nerves carry information in the form of electrical impulses from every part of the body to the brain and back. Via this intricate network of nerves – the body's communication network – the brain monitors and controls all your bodily functions.*

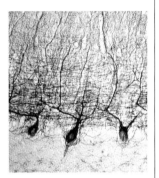

*Nerve cells are electrical messengers that transmit information to and from every part of your body.*

The nervous system divides into two parts: the central nervous system, which consists of the brain and the spinal cord; and the nerves that carry information to and instructions back from the central nervous system. The nerves are themselves organized into the peripheral nervous system and the autonomic nervous system. The peripheral system handles actions that are normally under conscious control, while the autonomic system regulates functions such as heartbeat.

Nerves are long fibres made up of chains of cells that conduct information in the form of an electrical current. Each nerve cell has a receiver and a chemical transmitter. This transmitter releases a chemical known as a neurotransmitter, which conveys the electrical signal to the receiver of the next cell, and so on.

## Types of nerve

There are two types of nerve in the body. Sensory nerves convey information to the brain, and motor nerves pass instructions back from the brain to the muscles. When impulses from the brain reach the muscles around a joint, muscle fibres shorten, moving the bones.

Although nerves send information to the brain via the spinal cord, they have no feeling themselves. When you feel the pain of a cut finger or a stubbed toe, you are "feeling" this in your brain, not in the affected part. All sensations happen in the mind rather than in the part of the body that is directly affected.

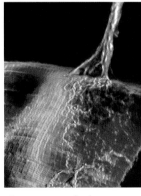

*A nerve attached to a muscle fibre conveys the signal that makes the muscle contract.*

## The spinal cord

Running from the base of the brain down the spine through the spinal canal, the spinal cord is the nervous system's "information superhighway". Along its length, nerves leave the cord through gaps between the vertebrae and branch out, forming a vast network. The spinal cord uses this network to collect impulses from all over the body, transmits the information to the brain and relays instructions back to the muscles.

The spinal cord does not extend along the whole length of the spine. It stops at the first lumbar vertebra in the lower back. From here, a sheaf of nerves, the *cauda equina* (Latin for "horse's tail"), continues downward.

## Protecting the spinal cord

The cord is protected by three meninges, or tubes of thin tissue, one inside the other: the pia mater, the arachnoid and the dura mater. The cord is itself an extension of the brain, and these membranes are continuations of the meninges that cover and protect the brain. The outer layer, the dura mater, is a flexible protective sheath. Inside this, the space between the two inner membranes is filled with cerebrospinal fluid, the liquid that bathes the brain.

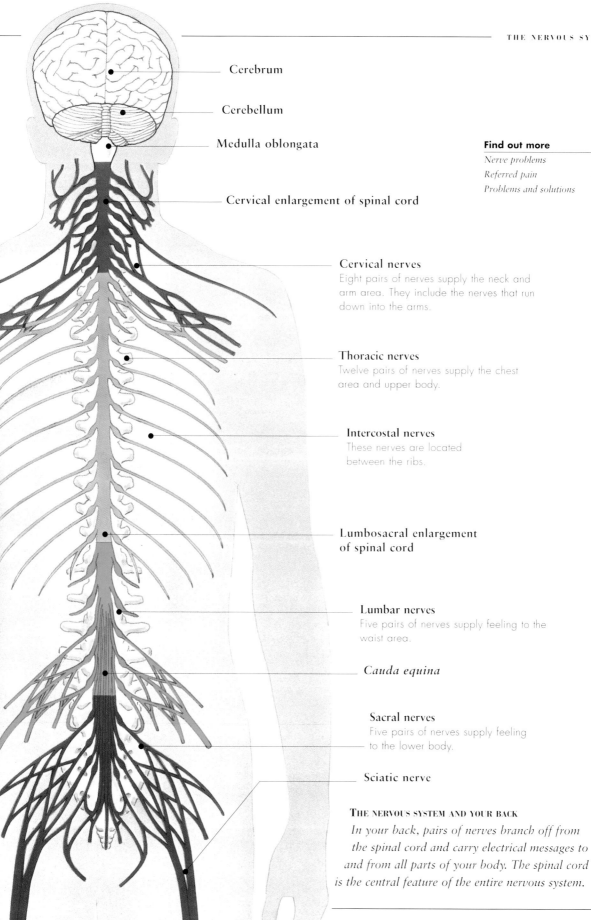

Cerebrum

Cerebellum

Medulla oblongata

Cervical enlargement of spinal cord

### Cervical nerves
Eight pairs of nerves supply the neck and arm area. They include the nerves that run down into the arms.

### Thoracic nerves
Twelve pairs of nerves supply the chest area and upper body.

### Intercostal nerves
These nerves are located between the ribs.

Lumbosacral enlargement of spinal cord

### Lumbar nerves
Five pairs of nerves supply feeling to the waist area.

### *Cauda equina*

### Sacral nerves
Five pairs of nerves supply feeling to the lower body.

Sciatic nerve

### THE NERVOUS SYSTEM AND YOUR BACK
*In your back, pairs of nerves branch off from the spinal cord and carry electrical messages to and from all parts of your body. The spinal cord is the central feature of the entire nervous system.*

# 2

# TREATING YOUR
# BACK WELL

Many people damage their backs in accidents, through sporting injuries or by lifting heavy loads the wrong way, but a large proportion of simple back pain is caused by the way a person sits, stands and walks. People often talk about "good" and "bad" posture but there is no proof that a particular position is always associated with back or neck pain. Posture is very much an individual matter – what is painful for you may cause another person no problems. This chapter gives general guidelines, but you need to try out various positions and find what suits you. This is well worth doing, because trial and error can, in the long term, be the key to a pain-free future.

# Sitting: how to sit correctly

M*ore and more people spend a large part of the day sitting down, whether at home or at work. The sitting position places more strain on the spine than either walking or lying down, so it is important to sit correctly if you are to avoid back pain. Well-designed furniture can help to keep your back fit.*

The spine has a natural S-shape that is most pronounced in the lumbar region – the area known as the small of the back. If you sit correctly, your spine naturally assumes this S-shape and most of your weight is supported by the bottom of the pelvis. But if you slump in your seat, the lumbar spine and pelvis form a C-shape, putting great pressure on the joints, discs and muscles of the lower back.

*A well-designed hard chair can be just as comfortable as a soft one, and will be more likely to encourage a sitting posture that is beneficial to your back.*

### Leaning forward

If your work involves a lot of reading, writing or bending over a desk, a sloping work surface such as those used by draftsmen and architects is ideal. If this is impractical, prop up your reading matter against a few books or filing trays. Leaning forward over a desk places great strain on the discs in your lumbar region.

### "Kneeling" chair

*A chair on which you "kneel" allows you to sit in a posture that preserves your back's natural S-curve and distributes your body weight evenly between your knees and buttocks. Some designs have an integral rocking action that allows for continual changes in posture.*

### The right furniture

Although many office workers spend up to 40 hours a week sitting in the same chair, some standard office furniture is not designed with the comfort of the back in mind. A good office chair needs to be fully and easily adjustable, and should work well with the rest of the furniture. The benefits of a new and supportive chair will be reduced if the arm rests prevent you from sitting with your legs under the desk or your feet flat on the floor, for example.

### Computer posture

If you work at a computer, the keyboard should be in front of the screen. Adjust your seat to place the keyboard roughly at elbow height while allowing your feet to rest firmly on the floor. Your forearms should be reasonably horizontal, and you should be looking slightly downward.

The seat should support your thighs, but the front edge should not dig into them. Adjust the backrest to support the small of your back. If your chair does not provide sufficient lumbar support, try placing one or two cushions behind the small of your back.

Looking down and sideways to copy from documents can lead to neck and back strain. Try using a copyholder to hold the documents beside the screen. ▶

**FICE DESK**

*ing incorrectly at a computer is a
nmon cause of back strain, but a few
iple precautions can reduce the risk.*

### Head position
Make sure the centre of the screen is
at, or just below, eye level. Raise the
screen on books if necessary.

### Arm position
Your forearms should
be reasonably level
with the desk.

### Elbow position
The elbows should
be approximately
below the shoulders.

### Foot position
Adjust the height of the seat
so that your feet rest firmly
on the floor.

### Seat depth
The front of the chair should not touch
the back of your knees.

# Sitting: how to sit correctly

### ▸ At home

The seeds of posture-related back pain are often sown as people sit at home, relaxing from the stress engendered by a hard day at work. The problem is that sofas and armchairs are designed according to the dictates of fashion rather than for the needs of the human back.

Sofas and armchairs can cause back problems if they are too soft, the seat is too low and too deep, or the backrest is too short. The spine's natural curve may need support in the lower back, or lumbar region, and much home furniture does not supply this.

A back-friendly easy chair allows you to sit with your lower back firmly against the backrest and both feet flat on the floor. The backrest should also be shaped to give some extra support to the lumbar region. If it is not, place a cushion or two behind the small of your back.

If the seat is too deep you either have to sit forward with your feet on the floor, a position that encourages you to hunch, or with your lumbar region against the backrest and your feet off the floor. In both these positions the spine adopts a shape that may bring on back pain. A seat that is too soft or too low also encourages you to sit in a position that puts excess strain on your spine.

### Neck hazards

Lying on your side with your head on the armrest of the sofa while reading, watching television or dozing is a habit that may lead to eventual strain. The angle of the armrest twists the neck, leading to neck pain. If you want to lie on your sofa in this way, always support your neck with cushions and try to change sofa ends every 30 minutes or so to even the strain.

**SITTING AT HOME**
*Much so-called comfortable furniture is not back-friendly. By applying the principles of good sitting and making use of cushions and boards you can help keep back problems at bay.*

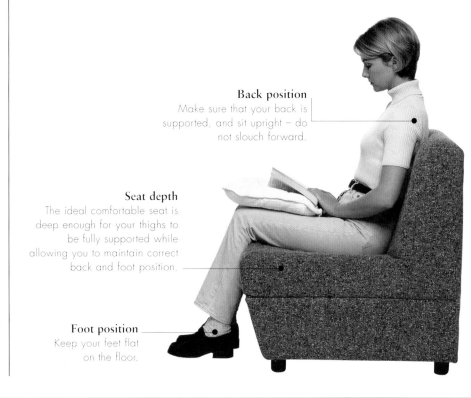

**Back position**
Make sure that your back is supported, and sit upright – do not slouch forward.

**Seat depth**
The ideal comfortable seat is deep enough for your thighs to be fully supported while allowing you to maintain correct back and foot position.

**Foot position**
Keep your feet flat on the floor.

*A chair or sofa seat that is too soft may be made firmer by placing a board – wrapped in foam – underneath. This may also raise the seat a little.*

## Adapting older furniture

It is not necessary to refurnish your home completely. You can take simple measures to improve your existing sofas and armchairs. If the seat is too deep, try placing several cushions behind your back. If the seat is too low, you may be able to have new, higher legs fitted by a furniture or upholstery shop. If the seat is too soft, wooden boards, wrapped in soft foam, can be placed beneath the seat.

## Watch your posture

Even the most supportive sofas and armchairs may not protect your back if you do not pay attention to your posture. Sit upright, make sure the small of your back is supported and keep your feet on the floor. The human body, and especially the human back, is not designed to stay in one position for long – our ancestors seldom had time for such luxury in a predatory prehistoric world. When reading or watching television, change your sitting position frequently – get up and move around every 30 minutes or so to stretch your back.

## Starting early

The principles of treating your back well apply as much to children as to adults. It is just as important for children to change their sitting position at frequent intervals. It is also vital that the furniture that they use fits them.

In many cases children have to make do with furniture designed for adults. If a chair is too high, support the child's feet with a box or even on a pile of heavy books. Work surfaces, especially desks or computer tables, are often too high for a child. This results in hunched shoulders and strained upper arms. If this is the case, raise the height of the seat. If this cannot be done, sit the child on a wedge-shaped cushion so that the keyboard is roughly at elbow level. With the thick part of the wedge at the back, the cushion will incline the child slightly forward. ▶

**Find out more**

| | |
|---|---|
| *Computer posture* | 22 |
| *In the car* | 26 |
| *Muscular problems* | 50 |

**CHILDREN AND COMPUTERS**
*By teaching the rules of sensible computer posture to your children, you can help them avoid problems in later life.*

**Screen**
The screen should be at about eye level.

**Seat back**
Pack the back of the seat with cushions for lumbar support if necessary.

**Seat height**
If the seat is too low, add some cushions so that she does not need to strain her arms upward.

**Foot position**
Make sure that her feet are flat on the floor.

# Sitting: how to sit correctly

### ▶ In the car

Some people spend a considerable amount of time in the car, either driving to and from work or on social and domestic journeys. Others, such as bus and delivery van drivers, spend their whole working lives behind the wheel. Yet how often does anyone choose to buy a vehicle because it is comfortable and back-friendly to drive? Private motorists choose their cars for performance, economy, fashionable body styling and even colour. Haulage companies and bus operators usually want the greatest possible carrying capacity combined with the maximum economy.

The general rules about sitting correctly in the office and at home also apply to sitting in your car or delivery van. If anything, it is more important to apply them here as, unlike in the office or at home, driving prevents you from changing your position significantly, often for long periods at a stretch.

Your seat should be firm and offer support for the lumbar region of the back. It should be adjusted to allow you to sit upright with your arms relaxed and not straining. Your legs should be comfortable, and you should be able to depress the clutch pedal – or accelerator if you drive an automatic – without overstretching. If the seat does not provide adequate lumbar support, use a cushion or fit one of the several types of manufactured support. If a headrest is fitted to your car seat, it should be adjusted to allow it to support your head in the event of a sudden stop or accident that could jerk your neck backward and forward, causing whiplash. If your car does not have a headrest, consider having one fitted.

## Checking your position

Try to sit upright with your chin tucked in rather than stuck out. Do not grip the wheel too tightly, try not to hunch your shoulders, and keep your head up. After driving for a few minutes, most people find they unconsciously slump down a bit. One way of keeping a check on this is to make sure you are sitting correctly when you adjust the driver's rear-view mirror at the start of the journey. In this way you will quickly notice any change in your posture as the mirror will appear to be wrongly adjusted.

Alter your position as often as possible, while still driving safely. Realistically, this means that you should not drive for long periods of time without taking a break. If you drive for your livelihood, do not stay sitting in the vehicle catching up with your paperwork or grabbing a quick snack during breaks between calls – get out and walk around to stretch your back.

**SITTING IN THE CAR**
*When buying a new car, more than the look of the vehicle, consider factors that will affect your posture. In the meantime, use a cushion if necessary to improve your posture.*

**Head position**
Make sure that your head is upright.

**Shoulders**
Do not hunch your shoulders.

**Back position**
Make sure you have enough lumbar support.

**Arm position**
Your arms should be comfortably bent in relation to the wheel.

**Foot position**
Make sure you can reach the pedals easily.

# Standing and walking

To help the spine cope with the strain caused by even gentle walking, it has its own shock absorbers, the intervertebral discs. But if the spine were a straight column of bones, the discs would only be able to absorb a limited amount of stress. Think about how vibrations travel up a wooden pole if you hold it upright and bang it on the ground. With a dead straight spine, even walking would be intolerable, let alone running or dancing. Instead, the spine's open curvature and cushioning discs make it strong, flexible and springy – an efficient vertical shock absorber. To maximize its effectiveness, it is important that you allow your spine to retain its natural shape by standing and walking correctly.

## Standing and walking tall
• Keep your posture as upright as possible. As you stand and walk, make an effort to keep straightening up. Some people find it helpful to imagine they are being lifted up by a rope or helium balloons attached to the top of their head.
• Keep your stomach in, your back straight and try not to hunch your shoulders. But it is just as important not to overdo it. Do not try to march around with your upper body rigid like a soldier on parade, as this can also cause strained and painful muscles.

## Losing weight
• If you are overweight, it will help if you can shed a few of the excess kilograms. Being overweight is generally bad for your health and puts stress on all joints, including those of the spine.

• Carrying extra weight on the front of the torso, in the form of a "beer belly" for example, shifts your centre of gravity forward. This puts a strain on the spine and results in hunched shoulders and an exaggerated curve in the lumbar area of the back. This is one of the reasons why so many women in the later stages of pregnancy suffer from back pain.

## Footwear and bags
• Your shoes can influence posture and have a bearing on back pain. Stiletto-type heels are the worst, but all high-heeled shoes may cause problems. They hollow the lower back, push the whole body out of alignment and strain the leg muscles.
• Well-cushioned, comfortable walking shoes with a heel of not more than 2.5 cm (1 in) are the most back-friendly footwear. For smarter shoes, choose a pair with heels that are less than 5 cm (2 in) high and try not to stand for long periods.
• If you wear trainers, always lace them. Wearing them unlaced causes you to curl your toes in order to grip the soles, transmitting tension through your legs and into your back.
• Heavy shoulder bags carried for any length of time on one side of the body or with the strap around the neck can aggravate postural problems. Change it regularly from shoulder to shoulder to equalize the strain on your spine and upper back. Use a small backpack instead or try dividing a heavy load between two bags.

*The combination of high heels and a heavy bag may well cause back pain. Choose low-heeled shoes and a small, light bag whenever possible to avoid straining your back.*

*Walk tall, as if you are being held up by a thread attached to the top of your head.*

# Daily routine

*Everyday life holds all sorts of hazards for your back. Some dangers are more obvious than others. Work-related injuries, for example, are a common cause of back pain. But even in your apparently secure home you constantly perform countless simple and mundane tasks that can damage your back.*

Bending, lifting and carrying correctly are an essential part of looking after your back. This means minimizing the strain on your spine by keeping your back as well aligned as possible. The bones and the discs of the spine can support your body weight and absorb stress very efficiently as long as the natural S-shape is maintained.

When you move away from the vertical and begin to bend, your centre of gravity shifts forward. This increases pressure on the discs of the spine and means that your back muscles have to

*A freestanding, adjustable shaving mirror placed on a shelf at a convenient height allows you to stand upright while shaving, and may help you to avoid low back pain.*

work hard to prevent you falling over. As a result, bending forward for any length of time in order to carry out household chores, duties at work or to grasp and lift heavy objects puts you at risk from pain.

## Housework

Many of the routine tasks in and around the home are potentially stressful for your back. But with care and planning, you can adapt your environment to protect yourself. The chart opposite gives some examples of common household chores and advice to help make them less likely to cause back injury.

## In the bathroom

Try to avoid bending over the washbasin for any length of time as this can be extremely stressful for the back. For men, shaving is an activity that can often cause low back pain. A mirror fixed to the wall behind the basin forces you to bend forward while you shave. In addition, many bathroom mirrors are placed at a comfortable height for the smaller of two partners – but this means that the taller one has to stoop as well as lean forward, so increasing the risk of back pain.

If you already have back problems, showering may be less stressful than taking a bath. You may feel fine soaking in a hot bath but getting out can be difficult. When washing your hair, kneel beside the bath instead of leaning over it.

## HOUSEWORK AND YOUR BACK

| | |
|---|---|
| BATH CLEANING | Bending forward over the bath puts stress on your back. Kneel beside the bath and use a long-handled brush to reach the far side. |
| BED MAKING | Kneel down or bend your knees keeping your back straight. Do not lean across to tuck in bedclothes, instead go round to the other side of the bed. Duvets and fitted sheets are easier to manage than blankets and flat sheets. |
| DUSTING AND POLISHING | Do not dust or polish above shoulder height. Use a stepladder to reach higher areas to avoid strain and pain in your upper back. |
| IRONING | When ironing, make sure that the board is high enough so that you do not have to stoop. If the board is too low even when fully extended, raise it on large, secure blocks of wood. |
| KITCHEN CUPBOARDS | Keep the most-used crockery, saucepans and utensils in cupboards that can easily be reached without bending or stretching. Store heavy objects, such as casserole dishes, at waist level so you do not have to lift them at awkward angles. To reach high cupboards use a stepladder. |
| KITCHEN WORK SURFACES | Ensure these are the right height to avoid bending. The ideal height is 5–10 cm (2–4 in) below elbow height. If the surface is too low, raise the unit on blocks. If it is too high, stand on a box or try library-type steps. |
| SWEEPING | Use a long-handled brush to avoid bending. Never bend over from the back when using a dustpan and brush. Squat or kneel, keeping your back straight. |
| VACUUMING | Keep the handle close to you and stand up straight. Use your legs and body weight rather than just your arms to move the machine around. |
| WASHING THE FLOOR | Use a long-handled mop for routine floor washing. Kneel on all fours if you are going to scrub the floor with a brush. |
| WASHING MACHINES | Kneel down to load and unload a washing machine. Place a clothes basket on a chair next to the machine and unload into that. This means you will not have so far to lift the full basket – wet clothes can be surprisingly heavy. When hanging out washing, lower the line to a comfortable height to avoid stretching or stand on a box. |
| WASHING THE DISHES | If the sink is too low and you find yourself bending, raise the height of the washing-up bowl by placing it on a stand or on an upside-down bowl. |

*Even with an ironing board at the correct height, little and often is a good rule for ironing so that you do not stand in the same position for too long at a time.*

# In the garden and do-it-yourself

*Gardening and do-it-yourself are hugely popular pastimes. For many people a few hours spent weeding or improving their homes provide a respite from the pressures of work. Yet more people damage their backs performing these tasks than doing anything else. A few simple precautions will protect your back.*

### Gardening

Looking after even a small garden can involve some relatively heavy manual labour – just the sort of activity that out-of-condition back muscles may not be able to cope with. All weekend you mow, rake, dig, weed and carry heavy loads. On Monday morning you feel stiff and by Monday night you cannot move for the pain from your aching back muscles.

For those with back problems and those wishing to avoid them, there are three basic rules for enjoyable gardening: keep your back as straight as possible, do not carry out any one activity for an extended period of time – always swap around between tasks – and do things at a comfortable pace. There is no point rushing to finish a job only to find you cannot get out of bed the next day.

## GARDENING AND YOUR BACK

| | |
|---|---|
| DIGGING | Grip the spade with one hand on the handle and the other near the blade. Keep your back straight, place a foot on the spade and push it into the ground using your weight. Use your knees rather than your back to lift out small amounts of soil. |
| HOEING, RAKING | Use long-handled garden tools to avoid bending. |
| MOWING | Keep the handles of the machine close to your body and use your weight, rather than your muscles, to move it. If you have a lot of cuttings or trimmings to dispose of, pile them on a plastic sheet and drag them to the compost heap. |
| WEEDING | Kneel rather than bend from a standing position, and always keep your back straight. A kneeling mat makes this job more comfortable. |
| WHEELBARROW | Avoid barrows with the wheel right at the front – this design means that you take most of the weight. If you have to use one, take small loads at a time. Better models have the wheel nearer the middle. |

*Use gardening tools with handles that are long enough to allow you to stand upright. If the handle is too long, saw some off: wrong use of the tool may also strain your back.*

## Do-it-yourself

The rules for gardening also apply to do-it-yourself, or DIY. Always use the right tools for the job, even if it means buying or hiring them. For back pain sufferers a good-quality adjustable work bench is invaluable. Adjust the worktop so you don't have to bend forward while sawing or planing. The key to back-friendly DIY is to take your time and to have frequent breaks. Because DIY is normally carried out in the evenings or at weekends, there can be a great temptation to push on to get the job finished. Resist this. You will do a better job if you do not rush, and no home improvement is worth a back injury that may last far longer than the day you saved.

*When lifting heavy objects in the garden, squat down with your knees bent and keep your back straight. Use your legs to lift, not your back, and always keep the object close to you.*

## DO-IT-YOURSELF AND YOUR BACK

| | |
|---|---|
| CARPETS | When laying carpets always work squatting, kneeling or on all fours. Do not bend over to pull, adjust or roll the carpet. |
| FLOORS | When mending or painting floors work on all fours or squat, keeping your back straight. A kneeling mat can make this more comfortable. |
| KITCHEN UNITS | Installing wall units: use a sturdy stepladder, not a kitchen chair. Do not climb up the stepladder and then bend down to lift up the unit. Ideally, ask someone to hand it to you. Position the steps to allow you to work as close to the job as possible. Low units: get down to the level of the job – sit or kneel on the floor as you work, do not bend forward from a standing position. |
| PAINTING | Always work well within your reach, do not bend or stretch. If using a ladder move it as you progress. Try to alternate the hand you paint with. |

*A good-quality work bench that can be adjusted in height is worth the investment, especially if you do a lot of DIY.*

# Lifting and carrying

*W*hen *you bend forward from the waist, the discs in your spine come under great pressure and your back muscles have to fight against both your own body weight and the pull of gravity. Then the muscles have to work even harder to pull you upright. This effect is compounded if you lift a heavy load from this position, and can easily result in a back injury.*

If you already have back problems, try to avoid lifting and carrying heavy loads. If this is not possible, learn to lift and carry correctly.

Position yourself close to the load with your feet on either side of it and one foot slightly in front of the other, facing the direction in which you want to go. Keeping your back straight, lower yourself down to the level of the load by bending at the knees and hips. Pick up the load, using handles if they are there or

with one hand below one side and the other at the front. With your body close to the load, lean forward slightly and then, keeping your back straight, straighten your knees and hips and stand up. As you lift, always keep the load close to your body, since holding something heavy at arm's length will cause strain. When lowering the load, reverse this procedure. Keeping your back straight, bend at the hips and knees and return the load to the ground.

**LIFTING HEAVY OBJECTS**
*Incorrect lifting is one of the prime causes of back injury. You can avoid problems by following a few simple rules when you lift or carry a heavy object.*

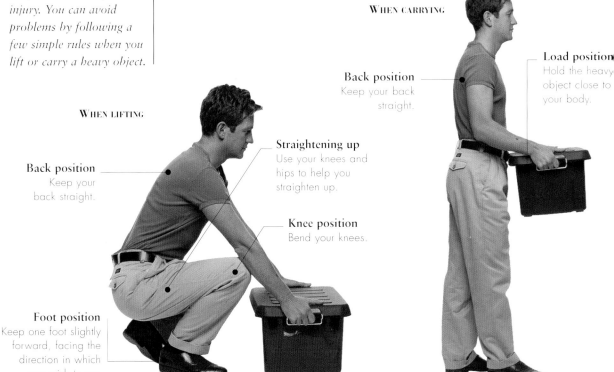

**WHEN CARRYING**

**Back position**
Keep your back straight.

**Load position**
Hold the heavy object close to your body.

**WHEN LIFTING**

**Back position**
Keep your back straight.

**Straightening up**
Use your knees and hips to help you straighten up.

**Knee position**
Bend your knees.

**Foot position**
Keep one foot slightly forward, facing the direction in which you wish to go.

*Using your shoulder as a support when lifting a long heavy weight keeps the load closer to your body and should help to minimize back strain.*

### Long heavy objects

If you have to lift a long heavy object, such as a roll of carpet, lift the end nearest to you then, straightening your knees and hips, stand up and, with the opposite end of the object still on the floor, walk toward it until the object is vertical. Help support the object with one hand halfway down its length and squat once more to grasp the bottom with the other hand. As before, straighten your knees and hips to stand up – always keep your back straight and the load close to you.

When carrying heavy objects, keep them close to your body at all times to keep your back straight. Break down heavy loads into more manageable weights if possible. It is better to make several journeys than to damage your back. If you are carrying heavy luggage or shopping, divide the load equally between two bags or between two bags and a backpack. If possible, use a luggage or supermarket trolley.

Lifting heavy loads out of the back of a car, especially if the boot is deep or has a high sill, causes many back problems. If possible, break the load down into smaller loads. When you are packing the boot, stow the heaviest loads closest to you to minimize bending. Avoid twisting while lifting objects.

### Hazards for parents

Lifting children from the floor and out of cots and pushchairs can also trigger back problems. New mothers are especially vulnerable, as hormonal changes during pregnancy cause the ligaments of the spine and pelvis to soften and stretch in order to ease the baby's head through the pelvis. It can take up to six months after the birth for them to return to normal. The advice about lifting heavy loads applies equally to lifting children – bend your knees to save your back. Never attempt to lift a child with your arms held out straight in front of you.

### Are you moving correctly?

• Always keep your back as straight as possible.
• Ensure work/kitchen surfaces are the right height to avoid bending forward.
• In the kitchen store heavy objects, such as casseroles, at waist level.
• Use long-handled brushes, mops and garden tools to avoid bending your back.
• Crouch or kneel rather than bend when polishing, dusting, cleaning the bath or making beds.
• Do not bend over the basin to wash your hair, kneel beside the bath instead or, better still, wash you hair in the shower.
• Try not to carry out any one activity for an extended period of time. Swap around between tasks.
• When lifting always hold objects (and children) close to your body, keep your back straight and flex your knees and hips to lift.
• Whenever possible, break down the load into smaller, lighter bundles.

*Don't get into the habit of bending over to lift children – instead, bend your knees and lift correctly, keeping your straight back.*

# Beds and backs

People spend up to a third of their lives in bed and yet, for many, "bed" means a sagging mattress on top of a dilapidated base unit. Over time, old or second-hand beds can allow the spine to sag and strain the muscles and ligaments of the back.

Many people fail to associate their back trouble with their bed, even though they often wake up feeling stiff and sore. A good bed will not cure your back problem, but it can help prevent it becoming worse and will increase your chances of a good night's sleep. If your bed is sagging, worn out or uneven, if you can feel the springs or if you and your partner roll together unintentionally, you should consider buying a new one. If that is not possible, you should take action to improve your old bed. If the mattress sags or is too soft, for example, and the bed has a sprung base try placing a board between the two.

## Looking for a bed

The ideal bed should be both supportive and comfortable. It should be firm enough to hold your spine level and allow ease of movement, but at the same time it should be soft enough to mould to the contours of your body and support its hollows and curves.

If you suffer from back pain the type of bed that will ease your pain depends very much on your individual needs. You will have to try out different beds to find the right one for you. When shopping for a new bed, remove your outdoor clothing and shoes and lie down on it for as long as possible.

Always take your sleeping partner with you and try the bed together – this will affect how it feels. Sharing a bed can be uncomfortable, particularly if you have back problems, if you and your sleeping partner are very different in size and weight. It might be better to consider two different single size mattresses, which can be zipped together, or even two separate single beds pushed together.

Buying a bed is probably one of the most important purchases you will make, so it is worth taking the time to get it right. Don't buy a bed in a hurry. Make notes on the beds you have tested – even those that do not seem suitable – and return another day to try them again. You may find that your perceptions have changed.

Some shops and manufacturers allow their customers to take a bed for a trial period, but this is not common and such beds tend to be expensive.

One final point: don't make the mistake of choosing a bed that is too hard – it can be as uncomfortable for back-pain sufferers as one that is too soft. Many manufacturers label their ultrahard beds as orthopaedic, but this has no medical status and does not relate to any agreed standard of firmness.

*Test out a bed for as long as possible before you buy to find out whether it is right for you. Lie in several different positions, as you do when you are sleeping. The right bed is supportive but also moulds to your contours.*

GOING TO BED

GETTING UP

*To get into bed when you have a bad back, sit on the edge of the bed, lower your body on to an elbow, draw up your knees and gently roll on to your back. To get out of bed, reverse this procedure.*

## A higher bed

Many back-pain sufferers find it easier to get into and out of a higher bed. Beds with storage drawers underneath tend to be higher, so choose one of them. Alternatively, many beds can be raised by attaching longer legs to the base unit.

## Pillows are important

It is essential to have a good, supportive pillow. Although there is the phrase "laying your head on a pillow", the pillow's job is to support the neck, helping to keep the neck vertebrae in line with those in the chest. Sleeping with too many pillows, or with a pillow that is sagging and worn out, can result in a strained and painful neck. If you do have neck problems, try using a "butterfly" pillow – similar to a travel pillow – which prevents your head lolling sideways if you sleep on your back. Once again, the pillow to suit you can only be found by experimentation – but it is worth making the effort to do so. As with beds, with pillows you tend to get what you pay for – the more expensive ones last longer and retain their shape better than poor-quality ones.

## Easing the pain

Some people with back pain find that lying on their back with one or more pillows or a piece of foam under their knees helps ease the pain and ensures a good night's sleep. This position tends to push the spine into the bed, preventing it from arching. Some people use a "sleep roll" made from a rolled-up towel. They wear it around their waist to create extra support for the lower back while lying on their back in bed. Alternatively, try lying on your side with your legs drawn up and a pillow between your knees. This position can be especially helpful for relieving the pain of sciatica.

If you have back pain, avoid painful twinges when turning over in bed by drawing your knees up into a foetal position before slowly rolling over. Allow the weight of your bent legs to carry you over on to your other side.

*A soft, rolled-up towel worn around your neck may help support your neck and avoid pain.*

# Travelling and your back

*Increasing numbers of people are travelling greater distances, either for work or holidays. The change of environment that travel brings is exciting, but the novelty of new surroundings can present difficulties for those with back problems.*

The very nature of travel means that you lose a large measure of control over your environment. As a result, the traveller is frequently forced to carry heavy luggage over unexpected distances, to sit for long hours in uncomfortable seats and to sleep in often unsuitable beds. With a bit of forethought, many of these problems can be overcome to ensure a pain-free trip.

## Packing

It is the oldest rule in the traveller's handbook and the one that is most often broken – do not pack too much. Carrying clothing and accessories for every conceivable occasion will not seem like such a good idea when you are staggering along in tropical heat under the weight of your luggage after an exhausting 12-hour flight.

Carrying a single, heavy suitcase for any length of time is almost guaranteed to cause back trouble. Equalize the load on your spine by dividing your luggage – take two small cases or two small cases and a backpack.

*Struggling with heavy luggage and sitting for hours on bad seating can place great strain on your back. It is better to travel with two small bags, evenly weighted, if possible.*

If you have to take a single large suitcase, buy one with stable wheels that you can pull along. You can also try using a folding luggage trolley – it can be checked in with your suitcase. The fact that your luggage has wheels should not provide an excuse to fill the case to the brim, as you will find that there may be extensive areas over which you have to carry it, for example up and down stairs. Make sure, too, that the case is not so tall that you have to bend your arms to keep the bottom from bumping on the ground. This puts excessive strain on the back.

## Travelling by air

Air travel holds many risks for those with back problems, beginning right at the start of your journey – in the airport. The seats in airport lounges usually have low backrests and little, if any, lumbar support. Some are the kind of plastic seats commonly used at bus stops.

If you have a long wait, use a rolled-up towel, sweater or coat to give you some lumbar support. Get up every 20 minutes or so and move around. Do some simple muscle stretching or go for a walk.

The standard seats on most aircraft are not usually particularly comfortable and the rows are often

*If two bags are not practical for travelling, choose a wheeled suitcase, but make sure it is inclined at such an angle that your arm is held straight.*

*In aircraft, rows of seats are often placed uncomfortably close together. When you are awake, get out of your seat every 30 minutes or so to stretch your legs.*

so close together that there is not much leg room. A cushion or folded blanket placed at the small of your back will give you some extra lumbar support, and the type of inflatable collar sold in most travel accessory and airport shops will provide support for your neck if you wish to go to sleep.

## Road and train travel

Travelling in cars, buses and trains is inherently stressful for the back as you are obliged to remain in the same seated posture for considerable periods of time. Even in a car with the best suspension, a continuous series of minor shocks and stresses are transmitted up the spine.

If you are making a long journey by car, try to build in time for frequent stops to allow you and your passengers to get out and move around. If you are a bus or coach passenger, make sure you get out and stretch your legs (and your back) at every available rest stop. On trains, get out of your seat every 30 minutes or so to exercise your back by strolling up and down the aisle.

## At the hotel

All sorts of unsuitable beds can lie in wait for weary and unwary travellers at the end of their journey. The most common problem is a bed that is too soft. If this is the case ask a member of the hotel's staff for a board to place under the mattress to firm it up. If it is a good hotel, this should not present too much of a problem for them.

If you suffer from low back pain and the bed is too soft or hard, try sleeping on your back with two pillows under your knees. Sleeping on your side with your legs drawn up and a pillow between your knees is another possible option. As an emergency measure, you can ask someone to help you drag the mattress on to the floor and sleep there – you can change rooms or even hotels in the morning.

If you are travelling by car and can carry more luggage, you could always take along a folding bed board, obtainable from specialist back shops, to improve a soft mattress. Beds that are too hard can be dealt with by packing a foam mattress topper or even a spare duvet.

*If you are away from home and suffering from back pain, pillows under your knees (above) or between your legs may help you to obtain relief.*

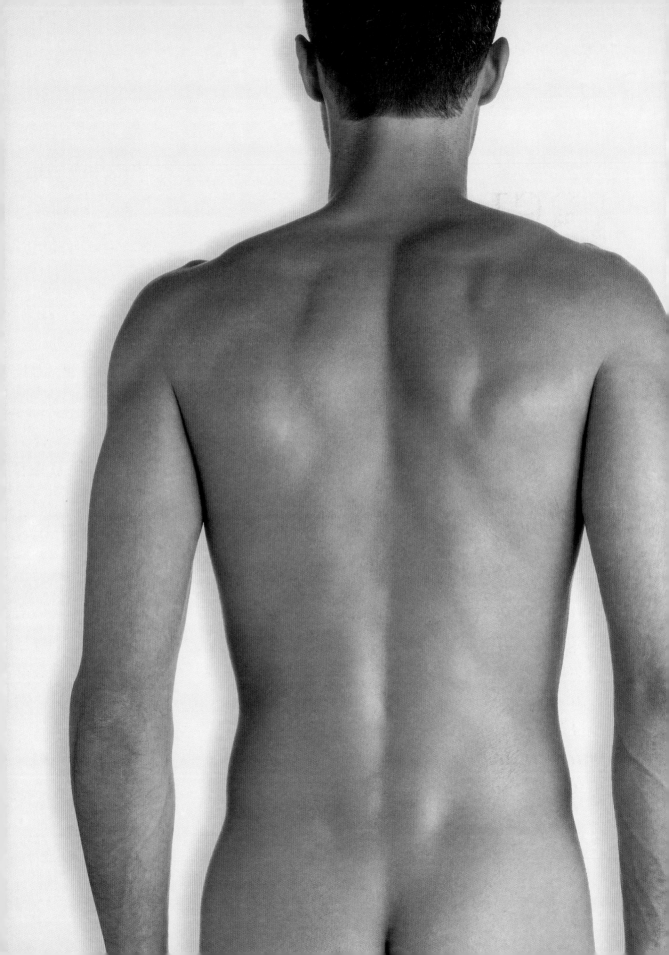

# 3

# ASSESSING BACK

# PROBLEMS

There are various ways in which the structures of the back can be damaged. Bones can be broken by a violent blow, sustained, for example, in a car accident or a fall from a horse. Muscles can be strained and sometimes torn during strenuous exercise. Other kinds of injuries can be the result of years of manual work. Damage can also be caused by degenerative disease, by malformation of the bones – and by simply growing old. In addition, back pain can be a symptom of other conditions.

This chapter describes the various problems and conditions that can cause back pain, together with advice on minimizing their impact.

CHAPTER THREE

# Skeletal problems

T*he most common cause of back pain is skeletal problems – problems affecting all the tissues of the spine other than muscles or nerves. If, like many people, you are not as fit as you could be, you run more risk of injury because your muscles will not be able to provide support when it is most needed.*

### Facet joint problems

Even normal everyday activities can force your back to work under great strain, putting extra pressure on your intervertebral discs. Injuries to the facet joints can occur in any part of the spine but they are more common in the lower back and neck regions where the facet joints have to withstand more twisting force, and possible strain, than elsewhere.

This type of injury is more common in middle and old age when the discs separating the vertebrae are beginning to dry out and become thinner. As a result, the spine becomes shorter, causing the ligaments that hold the vertebrae together to slacken. This can allow a facet joint to slip out of alignment under pressure. A misaligned facet joint can cause acute back pain, because irritation and bleeding within the joint cause the joint capsule to swell and press on a nerve.

The sacroiliac region, where the bottom of the spine joins the pelvis is a common problem site. The joints in this part of the back can be strained or pushed out of alignment by a sudden jolt – such as missing a step unexpectedly or sitting down too hard, especially on a seat that is too low. A violent, twisting motion may have a similar result.

### Effects of misalignments

If the problem is in your lower back you may also feel pain in your buttocks, hips and thighs. A facet joint problem in the neck will cause pain and restrict the amount of movement you can make. This is one of the causes of the condition known as wry neck. Facet joint problems may respond to rest, manipulation by an osteopath, chiropractor or physiotherapist. After the acute pain has subsided, exercise may help.

*The painful condition known as wry neck may be caused by a misaligned facet joint between vertebrae.*

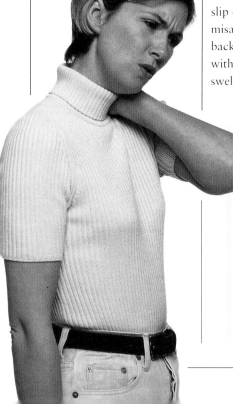

---

**FACET JOINT ALIGNMENT**

*Of all the joints in the spine, it is the little facet joints linking the rear of the vertebrae that are the most vulnerable to injury.*

NORMAL FACET JOINT

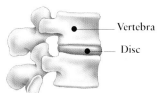

— Vertebra

— Disc

MISALIGNED FACET JOINT

— Misaligned joint

Many people with neck problems find that placing a soft collar or rolled-up towel around the neck helps provide support and eases the pain, allowing them to sleep better.

## Ligament problems

As well as slackening as a result of the normal ageing processes, ligaments – although pliable enough to allow movement around the joints – can become strained or, in extreme cases, torn. This is mainly due to the fact that ligaments in adults have very little elasticity. Torn or damaged ligaments take a long time to heal – even longer than bone. When they finally do heal, scar tissue often restricts the movement of the ligament across the surface of the bone, which may be a source of long-term inflammation and pain.

## Disc problems

The main sections of the vertebrae are joined to each other by the intervertebral discs. Although they are tough and their structure allows them to change shape temporarily under pressure, they can still be damaged.

The discs can absorb a great deal of vertical pressure, but they are vulnerable to sudden, twisting movements. This sort of movement can occur during some sports or through lifting heavy objects incorrectly. Damage is more likely to occur if the upper body is bent forward at the time, since in this position the facet joints are less able to prevent excessive rotation. If the vertebrae above and below a disc are suddenly forced to rotate in different directions, the outer casing, the *annulus*, can split – allowing the nucleus of the disc to bulge outward. ▶

## WARNING

*An awkward twisting or bending movement while lifting can cause injury to the intervertebral discs.*

## WHIPLASH

*A common cause of whiplash is an incident such as a car accident in which the head is jerked violently and unexpectedly forward or backward. As the muscles of the neck have no chance to prepare themselves for the impact, the joints are forced to the very limit of their movement and are only restrained by the ligaments. These can be badly strained or even torn by the force, causing internal bleeding between the neck vertebrae and the damaged ligaments. The symptoms of whiplash – pain and a very stiff neck – can take hours to appear and it is unlikely that the damage will show up on an X-ray.*

*Whiplash – or suspected whiplash – injuries should always be examined initially by a medical doctor to rule out any serious complications. Treatment includes rest and manipulation by an osteopath or chiropractor. Massage and acupuncture can relieve pain. Wearing a soft support collar (right) for the first couple of days can also help.*

# Skeletal problems

▶ This is what most people refer to as a slipped disc. Actually this is a misnomer, as a disc cannot slip out of place because the fibres of its outer casing are strongly woven into the substance of the vertebrae above and below. The medical term for this condition is a prolapsed disc. A prolapsed disc is more common in the lower back, although any part of the spine can be affected.

## Prolapsed disc symptoms

Discs have virtually no nerve supply of their own so the symptoms of a prolapsed disc vary according to which structures it bulges against. If it presses against nearby tissues and ligaments, acute pain may be felt at the site of the injury and a dull ache will spread out over a larger area. The pain will generally be confined to one side of the body – depending on the direction in which the disc is bulging. If the prolapsed disc presses against a nerve root, severe pain will often be felt in areas of the body that are served by the nerve, along an arm or leg, for example (see page 58).

Disc problems are more common in younger people. After middle age the discs, like most body tissues, begin to dry out – there is less nucleus to bulge out and interfere with other structures if the outer casing becomes damaged. If you do suffer from disc problems, the chances are that they will become less troublesome as you grow old.

If you suspect that you have a prolapsed disc, you should always seek conventional medical advice before undertaking any alternative therapy. Most disc problems resolve themselves with rest – which gives the nucleus a chance to shrink back to normal – however, osteopathy, chiropractic and acupuncture may help speed recovery and ease your pain.

## CASE HISTORY

When Jonathan, a 36-year-old teacher, arrived for his first consultation with an osteopath, his head and neck were locked over to one side and he was experiencing great pain. The osteopath spent the first part of the session taking a detailed history of her new patient. In the course of this, Jonathan mentioned in passing that he had driven to the osteopath's in his new car, which he had had to buy because his old one had been badly damaged in an accident a few months earlier.

Alerted by this, the osteopath asked for details of the accident.

Jonathan said someone had driven into the back of his car while he had been waiting at a traffic light. The car was a write-off but, amazingly, he had been unhurt. He had not even had to visit a hospital. The osteopath asked whether his neck problem predated the accident. Jonathan said that it had begun shortly afterward. Because he had been unhurt he had not associated the two events.

The osteopath diagnosed a chronic whiplash injury. After several sessions of treatment, the stiffness in Jonathan's neck disappeared. A year later, he has not suffered a recurrence of the stiffness and pain in his neck.

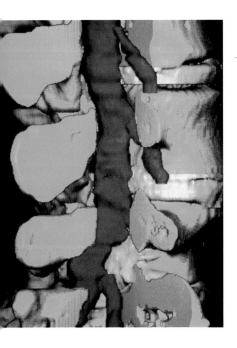

## PROLAPSED DISC

*When the bulging disc of a prolapsed disc impinges on the spinal cord it can cause severe back problems. In this false-colour X-ray, the disc at the bottom of the picture (yellow) is pressing on the patient's spinal cord (deep blue).*

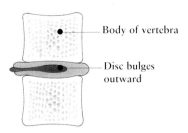

Body of vertebra

Disc bulges outward

## Bone problems

Most people think of broken bones in terms of some traumatic event, such as a car crash or a fall from a height. While these sorts of unexpected, violent accidents can easily injure the spine, sometimes in a life-threatening way, damage can also be caused by everyday activities. The bones of the spine can suffer a whole range of fractures, some so minor that they cause no symptoms and can only be discovered on an X-ray.

## Minor fractures

One of the more common minor spinal fractures is known as an avulsion, in which the tip of one of the transverse processes is cracked or pulled off. This can happen if a tendon attaching a muscle to the tip becomes overstretched and tears away, taking a bit of bone with it. This sort of injury is typically caused by some form of violent muscular action – sportsmen and women are the most frequent sufferers. Avulsions are characterized by severe pain as the injury occurs, and rest is the best treatment. If you do suffer from an avulsion, do not attempt any action that causes the pain to return until your back has healed.

Another common fracture is known as a microfracture. This is a small (sometimes very tiny) fracture that occurs in the weight-bearing bones of the spine. ▶

## AVULSION

Vertebra

Disc

*When a muscle tendon tears a piece off one of a vertebra's bony transverse processes, this causes an avulsion.*

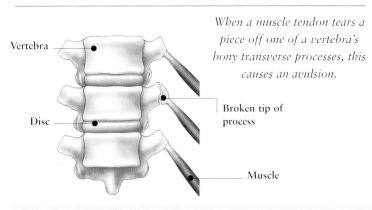

Broken tip of process

Muscle

# Skeletal problems

▶ A microfracture is normally caused by a violent, twisting action, typically as a result of a sports injury. But it can also occur in a more mundane manner – when incorrectly lifting a heavy load, for example. Rest is the best treatment.

## Crush fractures

When the spine suffers a blow that is too powerful for the discs to absorb, as in a poor parachute landing, a crush fracture – can occur. More usually, crush fractures can happen in old age as the bones lose their calcium and mineral content and become thin and fragile.

When a vertebra collapses, it generally does so more at the front than at the back. As a result the spine curves forward. This can cause the condition known as dowager's hump, in which an older person develops a hunched back. Rest and painkillers followed by drug treatment and calcium by mouth to remineralize the bones are the normal therapy in these cases. This halts the degeneration; physiotherapy and exercise may reverse the process to some degree.

## Spondylolysis

A fracture of, or gap in, one of the vertebral arches in the lower lumbar spine is known as spondylolysis. It can happen suddenly or as the result of a series of shocks and stresses, perhaps from years of long-distance running or gymnastics. Occasionally, the condition is hereditary. Spondylolysis often causes no symptoms at all and affected people may have the condition all their lives without being aware of it.

## Spondylolisthesis

This condition is often a progression of spondylolysis. In spondylolisthesis the vertebral arch breaks right through and the vertebra slides out of line with the rest of the spine – it usually slips forward. The condition can also occur if the facet joints wear down with age, allowing a vertebra to slip.

If the resulting misalignment is slight there may be no symptoms, but if the slipped vertebra presses against a nerve the result can be severe pain accompanied by tingling or numbness in the legs. Unlike other fractures of the spine, spondylolisthesis will not heal by itself and surgery may be needed to correct the problem.

## Scoliosis

The medical name for a very common sideways curvature of the spine, scoliosis can be the result of a structural defect or a response to a back injury such as a prolapsed disc.

One of the most common structural causes of scoliosis is having one leg slightly shorter than the other. These people learn to compensate by curving the spine toward the longer leg. This keeps their shoulders level and helps them avoid

### CRUSH FRACTURE

*Another name for a crush fracture is a collapsed vertebra, since part or all of the vertebral body may fracture in several places, causing the bone to collapse and the spine to curve forward. This can also force the facet joint to slip out of alignment. This type of injury may cause severe pain if a piece of bone presses on a nerve.*

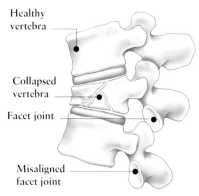

Healthy vertebra

Collapsed vertebra

Facet joint

Misaligned facet joint

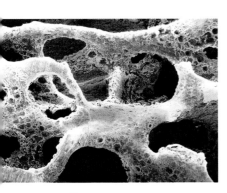

## OSTEOPOROSIS

*A microphotograph shows the fragility and sponginess of bones affected by osteoporosis – a condition that tends to be age-related – in which the bones of the body become brittle and prone to break.*

walking with a limp. However, the resulting unnatural curve of the spine makes it less able to absorb stresses caused by everyday activities and may leave it more susceptible to injury. After years of this posture the vertebrae can begin to wear unevenly, straining joints and causing pain.

Scoliosis that appears in childhood can be a serious condition. The vertebrae narrow on one side, causing the spine to lean toward that side and to rotate. It may be necessary for children with the condition to wear a brace while they are growing to prevent later deformity. In severe cases spinal surgery may be needed.

People suffering from back problems, for example a prolapsed disc, often adopt a pain-avoiding posture that causes the spine to curve sideways. This form of scoliosis tends to disappear as the injury heals and the pain recedes. Manipulation by an osteopath or chiropractor or physiotherapy and corrective exercises can be helpful in controlling this problem.

## AGE-RELATED BONE PROBLEMS

As people age, bone-related back problems may become more common. However, regular exercise and sensible precautions may help avoid problems.

### Osteoporosis

In the condition known as osteoporosis, all the bones of the body, lose much of their calcium and mineral content. This causes them to thin and makes them susceptible to fractures.

Although osteoporosis can affect younger people, it is mainly associated with ageing. It can strike men but women are the most at risk as the process of bone mineral loss speeds up after the menopause. Regular exercise, such as walking, running, aerobics or racquet sports, and a healthy, balanced diet rich in calcium and vitamin D are important in preventing osteoporosis. Research shows that those who remain active into old age are less likely to suffer. The most commonly prescribed conventional treatments are calcium by mouth and hormone replacement therapy, or HRT.

### Osteophytosis

Osteophytes are deposits of calcium, the building material of bone, which form spurlike growths on and around the vertebrae and may cause severe pain. They are a feature of osteoarthritis (also known as osteoarthrosis), a degenerative joint disease. ▶

*Regular load- or weight-bearing exercise, as well as helping older people to keep fit and active, slows the loss of bone density, and may offer protection against bone-related back problems.*

CHAPTER THREE

# Skeletal problems

▶ Osteophytis may produce no symptoms at all. But if an osteophyte grows into the gap through which a nerve root leaves the spinal column, or into the spinal canal itself, the sufferer can experience great pain.

## Spinal stenosis

A narrowing of the canal through which the spinal cord passes is termed spinal stenosis. It can be caused suddenly by a prolapsed disc or gradually by joint changes due to osteoarthritis and by the growth of osteophytes. It is more common in people who have a naturally narrower spinal canal and in those who have a vertebra which has slipped out of alignment with the rest of the spine.

Spinal stenosis is more common in the lumbar region. The narrowing that results from this problem can put pressure on the spinal cord and nerve roots. Symptoms can include pain, tingling and numbness in the legs that is made worse by standing erect and walking and relieved by sitting, squatting or bending forward. This is because the spinal canal widens when you adopt these positions. If you are overweight, losing the excess kilograms helps to relieve the symptoms. In serious cases, however, surgery to release the pressure on the spinal cord may be needed (see page 162).

If you experience pain in your back or legs accompanied by weakness or numbness or any loss of bladder or bowel control (sudden incontinence and/or loss of the normal feeling of wanting to go to the lavatory) seek medical help immediately as you may need urgent treatment.

## DISEASE-RELATED PROBLEMS

Other skeletal problems in the back are caused by diseases, mainly forms of arthritis, that can cause damage as the conditions progress.

## Ankylosing spondylitis

This fairly rare condition is also known as bamboo spine. It is a form of arthritis in which the joints of the spine gradually stiffen and lock rigid. Ankylosing spondylitis mainly affects young men and often runs in families. It normally starts at the sacroiliac joints and spreads slowly upward, although it can also spread down into the hips and, occasionally, into the other leg joints. In severe cases the spine locks permanently into a bowed posture.

To treat this disease, painkillers and anti-inflammatory drugs are prescribed, and exercises can help to keep affected joints flexible. Many people with the condition find that general exercise, especially swimming, is invaluable. Yoga exercises maintain general mobility and yoga breathing exercises, in particular, help open up the rib cage. Osteopathy, chiropractic and massage can also be beneficial.

---

### OSTEOPHYTES

*The bony spurs on vertebrae known as osteophytes may cause no symptoms. But if a nerve root becomes compressed, they may result in severe pain – or even paralysis of the muscle that the nerve controls.*

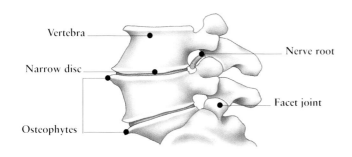

Vertebra

Narrow disc

Osteophytes

Nerve root

Facet joint

## Rheumatoid arthritis

One of the most common forms of inflammatory joint disease, rheumatoid arthritis normally affects joints symmetrically – both wrists and both feet, for example. The disease usually begins in the small joints of the hands and feet and progresses slowly to the larger joints, such as the hips and shoulders.

Rheumatoid arthritis does not usually affect the spine until many years after the condition has been diagnosed. When it does, however, it can cause a partial or complete dislocation of a neck vertebra. This complication makes manipulation of the neck – by an osteopath or a chiropractor, for example – potentially dangerous as it could result in a sudden compression of the spinal cord. Always fully discuss your medical history with a practitioner before any therapy begins.

## Paget's disease

This is a rare bone disease that causes the bones to thicken and deform. It usually affects all the bones in the body, not just the spine.

Although the condition can cause pain if a deformity squeezes a spinal nerve root, some sufferers do not even realize they have the disease. Most sufferers do not need treatment.

## CASE HISTORY

When Miranda, a civil servant in her early forties, moved home she decided to save on removal costs and did it herself with the help of friends. The following day she woke up in her new flat and found herself almost unable to move because of lower back pain.

As it was Sunday, Miranda spent the morning lying in bed with a hot water bottle at the small of her back waiting for the pain to go away. It didn't. By that evening she was only able to shuffle around using a chair as a makeshift walking frame. The next morning she managed to hobble to the doctor. She was advised to rest, prescribed powerful painkillers and told to come back in a week or so if things had not improved.

Miranda took the rest of the day off and telephoned a friend who had been treated by an osteopath a few months earlier. Miranda rang the osteopath and was given an appointment the next day.

He examined her and diagnosed a misaligned facet joint in the lumbar spine. He suggested that Miranda had probably done the damage by twisting her back while lifting pieces of furniture. The osteopath then gently manipulated Miranda's spine to realign the joint.

After that first visit Miranda found that the acute pain in her back disappeared, although it was still generally sore and stiff. However, after two more treatment sessions over the next few weeks she was completely free of pain. During her final visit, the osteopath gave Miranda advice on diet and exercises aimed at building up strength in her back and stomach muscles in order to help prevent future back problems.

# Skeletal problems at a glance

| PROBLEM | DESCRIPTION |
|---|---|
| ANKYLOSING SPONDYLITIS | Also called bamboo spine, this is a form of arthritis in which the joints of the spine gradually stiffen and lock rigid. In severe cases, the spine can become locked in a permanently bowed posture. |
| AVULSION | A fracture in which the tip of a transverse process, one of the bony protrusions at the rear of the vertebrae, is cracked or pulled off, often in the course of strenuous physical exercise. |
| CRUSH FRACTURE | The collapse of a vertebra. This can occur if the spine suffers a severe blow, in a bad parachute landing, for example, or as a result of bone-thinning due to osteoporosis. |
| DISC, PROLAPSED | Commonly known as a slipped disc. Damage to the disc's outer covering allows the interior to bulge out. Causes no symptoms unless it presses on a nerve or the spinal cord. |
| FACET JOINT PROBLEMS | Awkward, strained twisting movements, particularly when bending forward, can strain a facet joint or push it slightly out of alignment. Slack ligaments in the spines of older people can also allow facet joints to slip out of alignment. Can be a cause of wry neck or, if in the lower back, of lumbago. |
| FRACTURES | These can range from severe and life-threatening – for example when injury to the spinal column damages the spinal cord – to so minor that they cause no symptoms at all. |
| JOINT PROBLEMS | For many, the joints of the spine most likely to cause problems are the facet joints (see above) and the sacroiliac joints (see below). |
| LUMBAGO | The term used to describe pain in the lower back. Lumbago is not a diagnosis, it is a description of a symptom. |
| MICROFRACTURES | Tiny fractures that can occur in any weight-bearing bones of the spine. Can be caused simply by lifting a heavy load incorrectly. |
| OSTEOPOROSIS | A condition in which the bones of the body, not just the spine, become thin and brittle. It is a condition of ageing which speeds up in women after the menopause. It can result in crush fractures of the vertebrae. |

| PROBLEM | DESCRIPTION |
| --- | --- |
| PAGET'S DISEASE | A rare bone disease that causes bones to thicken and deform. It affects all the bones of the body, not just the spine. |
| RHEUMATOID ARTHRITIS | A common form of inflammatory joint disease that only normally affects the spine years after diagnosis. |
| SACROILIAC JOINT PROBLEMS | Sacroiliac joints link the bottom of the spine to the pelvis. They can be strained or pushed out of alignment by a sudden jolt or by a violent twisting motion. Expectant mothers or those who have recently given birth are particularly at risk. |
| SCOLIOSIS | A sideways curvature of the spine. It can either be a temporary posture in response to a back injury such as a prolapsed disc or, more seriously, a congenital condition. |
| SPINAL STENOSIS | A narrowing of the spinal canal through which the spinal cord passes. It can be caused by a prolapsed disc, joint changes due to osteoarthritis or the growth of osteophytes. The condition can put pressure on the spinal cord and surgery may be needed to relieve it. |
| SPONDYLOLISTHESIS | This is often a progression of spondylolysis (see below). The vertebral arch breaks right through and the vertebra slips out of line, usually forward. If the slipped vertebra presses on a nerve there can be severe pain, tingling or numbness in the legs. In serious cases surgery is needed. |
| SPONDYLOLYSIS | A fracture in the vertebral arch in the lower lumbar spine. It can happen suddenly or as the result of a series of shocks and stresses, after years of long-distance running for example. It often causes no symptoms. |
| WHIPLASH | This occurs when violent head movements, in a car crash for example, strain or tear the ligaments supporting the bones in the neck. The pain and stiffness of whiplash can take a number of hours to appear. |
| WRY NECK | Pain and restricted movement in the neck, which may be caused by a facet joint or disc problem. |
| NOTE | **The information and recommendations given in this book are not intended to be a substitute for medical advice. Consult your doctor before acting on any of the suggestions in this book.** |

# Muscular problems

*I*njuries *to the muscles of the back occur in many ways. Because the muscles are an integral part of the structure of the back, supporting the bones of the spine and controlling their movements, they are inevitably affected when injuries happen.*

If a facet joint slips out of alignment or you suffer a prolapsed disc, the muscles around the damaged area can become strained and painful as they struggle to support structures that are no longer in balance.

Muscles can be strained by postural stress or by any repetitive action carried out over a lengthy period of time. Damage also occurs when muscles are called upon to perform at the limit of their ability without preparation – strenuous exercise without a proper warm-up, for example. Psychological stress, too, manifests itself in tense and painful muscles (see page 52).

*The false-colour areas (left) represent muscle. There are more than 650 voluntary muscles in the body, many of which work in pairs. This means damage to one muscle may put strain on another, doubling your discomfort.*

## Structural damage

The role of muscles is to move the bones at the joints. To achieve this, the bundles of fibres that make up your muscles are able to contract and relax. When an injury occurs to any particular structure – a facet joint for instance – the muscles supporting and controlling it act immediately to prevent any further movement in case more damage is caused. To achieve this they contract, immobilizing the injured part in a vicelike grip – a muscular spasm. While a muscular spasm effectively immobilizes the injured area, it can also trigger a painful vicious circle. As long as the muscles are contracted in a spasm, they cannot be supplied with sufficient oxygen and this in itself causes pain. If the contracted muscles are also pressing on a nerve, even more pain is caused. The

*Stretching before sport allows the joints to start working freely, making them more pliable. This helps to prevent muscular injury.*

effect of this pain is to encourage the muscles to contract further, and so on. The longer a spasm goes on, the more difficult it is to break the cycle. However, for the injured joint to heal, the muscles must first relax. Massage, manipulation and relaxation techniques can help.

## Postural stress

Muscle strain as a result of poor posture is responsible for a significant proportion of back pain. Performing everyday activities with a good posture means that the various forces acting on the body are balanced and the muscles of the back do not have to work unnecessarily hard to keep things that way. But if you habitually slouch as you walk, sit badly at work and relax by sitting on poorly designed or ill-fitting furniture, your body is permanently off balance and the back muscles are placed under continuous strain. After a while, the muscles can become chronically tense and painful.

Although massage and manipulation help to ease cramped and aching muscles, unless the underlying problem is addressed the pain will most probably return. If you suffer from back pain for which there is no obvious structural cause, it is worth taking some time to investigate both your posture and your environment at home and at work. While few people can completely change how they live and work, there are plenty of ways in which their existing surroundings can be adapted to become more back-friendly.

## Repetitive actions

Another common cause of posture-related pain is carrying out any repetitive action using the same set of muscles for an extended period of time. Factory workers who have to perform the same task many times throughout the day are particularly prone to this problem. Cleaning or DIY sessions at home can also present this sort of risk. Try to balance the strain by using groups of muscles on both sides of your body whenever possible. For example, any period of repetitive action using your right arm should be followed by a session using your left. ▶

*Painting frequently causes upper back and neck strain. Change hands every so often to even the strain on the muscles of your upper arms and upper back.*

# Muscular problems

## CAN FOOD AND DRINK CAUSE MUSCLE PAIN?

*Some back-pain sufferers find that reducing the amount of tea and coffee they drink, or cutting them out of their diet altogether, helps to relieve or ease their symptoms. Both tea and coffee stimulate the nervous system. This can make your muscles tight and tense.*

*There is also growing evidence to suggest that some people suffer aching and painful muscles throughout the body as a result of an allergy to a particular food. In such cases cutting out the substances responsible can result in a dramatic improvement in symptoms.*

*There are various methods of testing for allergies but perhaps the most straightforward is the exclusion, or elimination, diet. This involves following a diet, normally for about two weeks, which excludes the most commonly troublesome substances. They are then reintroduced one by one to see if there is any adverse reaction. However, if you intend to cut out several items it is important to seek advice from a suitably qualified practitioner, such as a dietician or nutritionist, to ensure you are still eating a properly balanced diet.*

*A proper warm-up can reduce the risk of muscle strain, but cannot eliminate it. Professional athletes risk injury every day, from excess strain or sudden twisting movement.*

### ▶ Muscle injury

Although in everyday life a lot of back pain is attributed to strained or "pulled" muscles, muscles are not often injured in isolation. When they are, it is usually as a result of activities such as vigorous sports without proper warm-up or poor heavy lifting technique.

Prevention is always better than cure. Be sure to warm up and stretch before exercising. Warming up gets the cardiovascular system working efficiently. This in turn allows the joints to start working freely, which increases the flow of synovial fluid around them, making them more flexible.

Strained muscles can be very painful but normally heal naturally with rest. When the injury has healed, manipulation by an osteopath, chiropractor or physiotherapist can help restretch muscles that have become stiff.

### Psychological stress

Sometimes muscular pain in the back and neck has its roots in psychological causes. This does not make the pain any less real. The pain is just as valid and is caused by real muscular tension. The difference is that the muscular tension is caused by the emotions, not by structural damage or a sports injury.

When a person is angry, frustrated or frightened, the body produces chemicals that tense the muscles ready for action. These are the so-called fight or flight hormones. Without them early humans would not have survived in a violent prehistoric world.

Today the body works in the same way but the world is a different place. A person still feels anger and fear but the tension in the muscles is no longer released by fighting a neighbour for food or by fleeing from a predator. Instead, the feelings are turned inward because there is no physical action that can be taken to change the things that are causing the upset. As a result, the person may sit tense and fuming in the office or car unable to give vent to anger and frustration.

## Bottling it all up

If these bottled-up feelings are not released, the muscles may become chronically tense and painful. Stress of this type affects everyone in physically different ways. Some people suffer neck pain, others develop painful shoulders and arms and still others find their lower back seizing up in a spasm.

Experts believe this psychological element in back pain also helps explain how some people can carry out physically stressful repetitive tasks for years without developing muscle pains while others can become disabled. If your muscles are already tense because of troubles at home or job frustration you will be less able to tolerate physical strain than someone who is relaxed and happy.

### Find out more

## CASE HISTORY

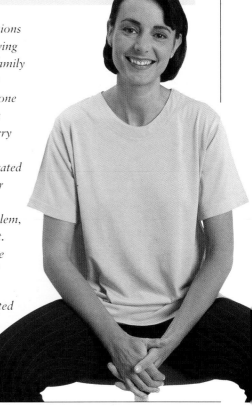

*Mary, 28, had been working as a sub-editor on a magazine for a year when she began to suffer from pains in her arms and shoulders. Her job involved spending hours at a computer editing news and articles produced by staff and freelance writers.*

*Despite paying attention to her posture and taking frequent "screen-breaks" away from her computer, Mary's pain gradually became more severe. Eventually, she was forced to start taking time off work. In desperation, Mary consulted her family doctor. He examined her but could find nothing physically wrong. The doctor offered to refer Mary to a counsellor who was attached to the practice. Mary reckoned she had nothing to lose and agreed.*

*Over the course of several sessions it became clear that Mary was having problems coping with a difficult family relationship. She had decided that there was nothing that could be done to improve the situation and, on a conscious level, had ceased to worry about it. The problem was that, subconsciously, she was still frustrated by the situation and as a result her muscles had become tense.*

*Once she understood the problem, Mary could do something about it. Although she could not resolve the situation, she could learn ways of dealing with the stress it caused. Mary learned meditation and started to practise yoga and within a few weeks her pain lessened, then finally disappeared.*

# Nerve problems

*The central feature of the nervous system in the back is the spinal cord and the nerves that branch off it. Although well protected, the nerves and spinal cord can sustain injuries. These injuries can, in turn, cause severe pain in your arms or legs.*

Pairs of nerves leave the spinal cord through foramena (gaps) between the individual vertebrae and branch out into fibres that reach into every area of the body. These nerve fibres are divided into two categories: sensory fibres that transmit sensations, such as pain and pleasure, to the brain, and motor fibres that carry instructions from the brain to the muscles.

Nerve problems in the back normally have a structural cause. The nerve roots can easily be squeezed as they leave the spinal cord by injuries to a facet joint or a disc. When this happens there may be local inflammation and pain but there can also be pain in any area of the body which is supplied by the affected nerve, for example down a leg or along an arm. There may also be numbness, or the prickling sensation of pins and needles.

*The sciatic nerve is the largest in the body, extending from the lower back down the back of the leg to the calf. Many sciatica sufferers find that lying on their side with a pillow between their knees gives them relief.*

## Sciatica

Pressure on the nerve roots commonly cause the condition of sciatica – the term means pain in the legs. If a nerve root is compressed, you may feel pain in your lower back, one buttock and down the outside or back of one leg as far as the calf. There may also be numbness and the tingling of pins and needles. The nerve roots carry both sensory and motor fibres so, in severe cases, there may also be weakness of the muscles in the leg.

Sciatica is a relatively common nerve root problem, since the facet joints and discs in the lower spine are more prone to injury than those elsewhere. At first, the pain may be worse in the lower back than in the leg, but after a few days the leg pain may be dominant.

Bed rest may be unavoidable in the acute phase of sciatica, but should be for

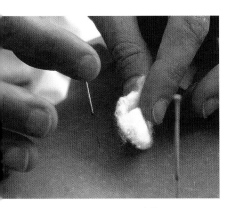

*Acupuncture treatment modifies pain signals to the brain, with the result that many sufferers have found that it eases the pain of sciatica.*

as short a time as possible. Most cases clear up within a few months as the structural injury heals. Massage, acupressure and manipulation by an osteopath or chiropractor can ease pain and speed recovery. Treatments include painkillers and anti-inflammatory drugs. In severe cases, surgery may be needed.

## Arm pain

Nerves leave the spinal cord at the base of the neck and run down the arms to the hands. As with sciatica, pressure on the nerve roots can cause pain and numbness or pins and needles along the arm. This condition is known as brachialgia. Muscle weakness may also be present. Massage, acupressure, osteopathy and acupuncture can all help. It is treated conventionally with painkillers and anti-inflammatory drugs. In severe cases a neck collar and traction or surgery may be needed.

## Nerve root fibrosis

Nerves leaving the spinal cord are encased in a protective membrane, or dural root sleeve. Occasionally, if the pressure on a nerve root has caused inflammation, scar tissue can form on the sleeve. This can "glue" the sleeve to the walls of the spinal canal, to a vertebra or even to nearby ligaments. Known as nerve root fibrosis or arachnoiditis, this sort of scar tissue can also form after surgery to correct a structural problem such as a severely prolapsed intervertebral disc.

In this situation, even when the injury heals and pressure on the nerve disappears, the nerve will be prevented from moving freely through the gap between the vertebrae in normal movements of the spine and limbs. This means that the pain from sciatica may disappear only to return when you bend forward because the "glued" root sleeve prevents the nerve from following the bending movement of your spine and limbs.

The pain of nerve root fibrosis usually disappears when you straighten up or lie down flat. Sometimes a "glued" root sleeve gently works itself free over time and normal movements can be resumed. If not, physiotherapy exercises may help to stretch the scar tissue. ▶

---

### NERVE ROOTS

*Pairs of spinal nerves attach to the fabric of the spinal cord both ventrally (at the front) and dorsally (at the back). The entire structure is protected by the layers of the arachnoid and dura mater.*

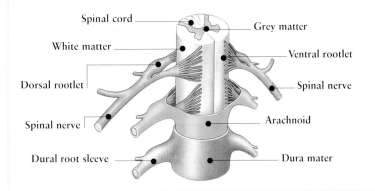

Spinal cord — Grey matter
White matter — Ventral rootlet
Dorsal rootlet — Spinal nerve
Spinal nerve — Arachnoid
Dural root sleeve — Dura mater

# Nerve problems

## ▶ Compression of the *cauda equina*

The *cauda equina* is a sheaf of nerves which fans out from the base of the spinal cord in the lumbar region of the spine. (The term means "horse's tail" in Latin, because of the nerves' resemblance to coarse, flowing strands of hair.)

If a disc in the area of the *cauda equina* prolapses backward into an already narrow spinal canal, the nerves of the *cauda equina* itself can in turn become compressed.

It is rare for this to happen, but it can have serious consequences. Characteristic symptoms are back and leg pain accompanied by weakness, numbness and disruption of bladder and bowel functions. If you suffer from any of these symptoms you should seek medical help immediately.

## Injury to the spinal cord

Although the spinal cord is well protected by layers of membranes that cushion it, if the spinal column is fractured by a violent blow or other form of physical injury, such as a bad car accident, the cord can be damaged. If this happens the results can be extemely serious and even life-threatening, depending on the type and location of the injury. If the damage is severe, paralysis can occur.

Any paralysis that does happen is likely to be permanent as an injured spinal cord cannot heal itself. The higher up the cord serious injury occurs, the more extensive the paralysis will be. A serious injury in the neck area is often critical because it can affect the nerves that control breathing, as well as causing paralysis in all four limbs.

## NERVE PROBLEMS

| PROBLEM | DESCRIPTION |
| --- | --- |
| ARM PAIN | Pain in the arm and/or hand can be caused by compression of a nerve or nerve root. It may be accompanied by numbness or pins and needles. In severe cases, there may be muscle weakness. |
| CAUDA EQUINA COMPRESSION | Back and leg pain accompanied by numbness, weakness and disturbance of bladder and bowel functions. This can be caused by a prolapsed disc bulging backward into the spinal canal. Seek medical help at once. |
| EPIDURAL ABSCESS | Back pain accompanied by fever and extreme tiredness. Caused by an infection around the dural tube of the spinal cord. |
| NERVE COMPRESSION | Pain in any area of the body served by the nerve. Can be accompanied by numbness or pins and needles and, in severe cases, by muscle weakness. Caused, for example, by pressure on a nerve or nerve root, by a prolapsed disc or damaged facet joint. |

## Infections

Although the great majority of nerve problems in the back have a structural cause, some can be the result of bacterial or viral infections.

The scar tissue that causes problems in nerve root fibrosis, or arachnoiditis, can result from inflammation caused by an infection. Infection can also cause an epidural abscess in which pus builds up in the spinal canal around the dural tube of the spinal cord. An epidural abscess normally produces additional symptoms, such as fever and extreme tiredness.

In rare cases, back pain can also be caused by meningitis. This is either a viral or bacterial infection of the meninges, the membranes surrounding the brain and spinal cord, protecting the brain and holding a network of blood vessels. The symptoms of meningitis – a stiff neck and back, severe headache, fever or chills and vomiting – often develop rapidly. The most common form is viral and this usually clears up by itself with bed rest and plenty of fluids. Bacterial meningitis, if diagnosed quickly, is effectively treated with antibiotics.

*A microscopic view of brain tissue infected by bacterial meningitis. This can be fatal if not treated immediately: see your doctor at once if you develop symptoms.*

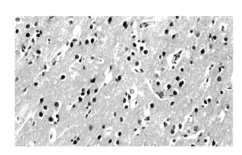

## NERVE PROBLEMS

| PROBLEM | DESCRIPTION |
|---|---|
| NERVE ROOT FIBROSIS | Pain on extending the spine, for example bending forward. The pain is usually relieved by straightening up again. It can occur when inflammation caused by compression or infection leaves scar tissue on the dural root sleeve of a nerve. The scar tissue can "glue" the sleeve to the side of the spinal canal, making it impossible for the nerve to move smoothly in and out between the vertebrae in response to movements of the trunk and limbs. Also known as arachnoiditis. |
| SCIATICA | Pain down one leg. It can be accompanied by numbness or pins and needles. It may be caused by compression of a nerve root, perhaps by a prolapsed disc. |
| SPINAL CORD INJURIES | Symptoms can range from bladder and/or bowel dysfunction, numbness and muscle weakness to paralysis. |
| NOTE | The information and recommendations given in this book are not intended to be a substitute for medical advice. Consult your doctor before acting on any of the suggestions in this book. |

CHAPTER THREE

# Referred pain

*P*ain is the body's warning system. It tells you something is wrong and prompts you to take action to tackle the problem. Sometimes the sensation appears to come from an area of the body other than the source of the pain.

*Reflex actions protect you from injury. The reaction of withdrawing your hand from a hot pan happens before you have time to think about it.*

If you accidentally try to pick up a hot saucepan, you feel pain in your hand and quickly snatch it away. The nerves in your hand flash a warning to the brain via the spinal cord that damage is occurring and the brain replies by telling the muscles to move the hand out of danger – fast. The pain is not really in your hand, it just feels that way. This is because the nerve supplying the hand, like all nerves in the body, has no "feeling" of its own. Its job is to transmit information in the form of an electrical current to the brain. The brain then interprets that information and labels it "pain". Because the pain signal is being transmitted by the nerve which supplies the hand, the brain labels it "pain in the hand" and that is how you consciously experience it.

This system normally works very efficiently but, in certain circumstances, it can lead to confusion. If, for instance, the root of the nerve that supplies the hand is compressed by a structural problem such as a prolapsed disc, the pain may be felt in the hand, not in the neck, where the disc actually is. This is because as far as the brain is concerned the nerve sending back the warning signal is the one that supplies the hand, so it labels the warning "hand pain". This is known as referred pain. Referred pain explains how "ghost pain" can occur. This is

when people who have had limbs amputated frequently feel pain in the part of their body that is no longer there. The remainder of the nerve that used to supply the amputated arm or leg goes on sending its warning to the brain and the brain goes on labelling this message as arm or leg pain.

In the human back, referred pain can be felt anywhere along the pathway of a compressed nerve. If one of the nerves that run from the base of the neck to the hands is compressed, pain can be felt down the arm and into the hand. If one of the nerves that run from the base of the spine down the legs and into the feet is compressed, pain may be felt in a buttock, a leg or even a foot.

The site of the referred pain can give doctors and therapists valuable information about exactly where in the back the troubles lie. If you feel pain in the back of a thigh and down the outer side of your leg and foot, for example, the problem may be in the base of the spine at the level of the sciatic nerve roots. Pain in a buttock or in the groin may point to a problem at waist level, and pain down an arm may indicate compression of a nerve root in the upper chest or neck region of the spine.

## Trigger points

Small areas of muscle that have become chronically tense, perhaps following an injury, years of poor posture or even as a result of bottled-up anxiety, anger or frustration are known as trigger points.

The muscle fibres at these points are in a state of constant spasm and often radiate pain to areas far away. A trigger point in the lower back, for example, can cause pain in a buttock. Sometimes the trigger point is far less painful than the target area. Many people have back pain triggered by chronic muscle tension elsewhere, in the neck or shoulders perhaps, of which they are completely unaware. In such cases, the trigger point remains "silent" until or unless it is revealed by a manipulation therapist's probing fingers.

## Other causes of referred pain

Just as structural problems in the back can refer pain to other areas of the body, disorders elsewhere can cause pain in the back. In these cases, however, there are usually other symptoms as well. If your back pain persists and is accompanied by any of the other symptoms listed on pages 60–61, consult your doctor as soon as possible, as you may need urgent medical attention.

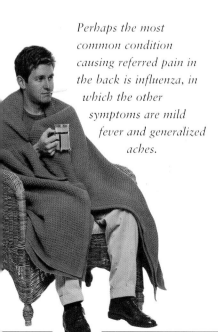

*Perhaps the most common condition causing referred pain in the back is influenza, in which the other symptoms are mild fever and generalized aches.*

*Modern medical technology offers an alternative to surgery for kidney stones. High-intensity ultrasonic pulses break up the stones, allowing them to be passed harmlessly in the urine.*

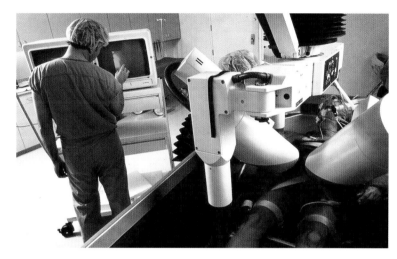

### Kidney problems

Your kidneys are responsible for filtering out waste products from your blood. Occasionally, deposits of hard mineral salts, or kidney stones, can form or the kidneys can become infected. Low back pain can be one of a number of symptoms in both cases. Kidney stones generally cause intermittent sharp pain in the lower back, along with nausea. Constant low back pain extending into the groin, accompanied by fever and discoloured urine may indicate a kidney infection.

### Gall bladder problems

The gall bladder concentrates bile secreted by the liver, before passing it into the digestive system, where it helps fat absorption. If too many stones of mineral salts form in the gall bladder, it may become inflamed. Pain is often felt in the lower tip of a shoulder blade, accompanied by abdominal pain, nausea and fever. ▶

# Referred pain

### ▶ Pancreatitis

The pancreas lies on the left-hand side of your abdominal cavity, near your stomach. It has two roles: producing enzymes, that are important for the digestion of food; and manufacturing the hormone insulin, which regulates the amount of sugar in the blood. Heavy alcohol consumption can result in the pancreas becoming inflamed, a condition known as pancreatitis. This can cause pain in the top of the stomach and an intermittent, gnawing pain in the mid-back. This is sometimes accompanied by diarrhoea and, occasionally, by jaundice (yellowing of the skin).

### Duodenal and stomach ulcers

Both the stomach and the duodenum – the tube that carries half-digested food from the stomach to the small intestine – where the process of digestion continues, can develop ulcers. The walls of both the stomach and the duodenum are protected from the strong gastric juices that digest food by a lining of mucus-producing tissue. If this lining wears away or is infected by *H. pylorii* bacteria, an ulcer – a patch of raw and sometimes bleeding tissue – can form. The result is often a burning pain in the mid-back or lower back area that can become worse after eating, especially spicy foods.

## REFERRED PAIN

| LOCATION OF PAIN | POSSIBLE CAUSE |
| --- | --- |
| Pain in the back of the thigh and/or down the side of the leg and/or foot. Possibly also pins and needles and a patch of numbness. | Compressed lumbar nerve root |
| Pain in the arm and/or hand. Possibly also pins and needles and a patch of numbness. | Compressed nerve root in the neck |
| Pain in buttock or groin. | Compressed nerve root in the upper lumbar area of the spine |
| Back pain with generalized aches and mild fever. | Influenza |
| Intermittent sharp low back pains with stomach pain and nausea. | Kidney stones |
| Constant or severe low back pain, fever and discoloured urine. | Kidney infection |
| Pain in the lower tip of a shoulder blade, colicky stomach pain, possible fever and shaking. | Gall bladder inflammation or stones |
| Intermittent gnawing mid-back pain, pain in the top of the stomach, possible jaundice. | Pancreatitis |

## Gynaecological problems

Menstruation and disorders of the female reproductive organs often refer pain to the lower back. Menstrual cramps, and premenstrual tension (PMT) can cause a dull, generalized low back pain. Infections of the womb and/or Fallopian tubes can also cause back pain in the lumbar area, usually accompanied by stomach pain, vaginal discharge and/or pain during sexual intercourse. A prolapsed womb may occur if the womb's supporting ligaments stretch, allowing it to drop into the vagina, which can cause a dull, dragging pain in the lower back. In this case immediate medical attention is necessary.

## Pneumonia and pleurisy

Pneumonia is an infection of one or both lungs, and pleurisy an inflammation of the membrane around them. Both can cause back pain and pain around the lower ribs. You may also have referred pain in the shoulder. Other symptoms are a cough, pain on inhaling and fever.

## Heart attack

Back pain can accompany a heart attack. There will also be severe, crushing chest pain, spreading to the jaw or down one arm. Other symptoms are breathlessness, dizziness, nausea, palpitations, feeling faint and cold.

## REFERRED PAIN

| LOCATION OF PAIN | POSSIBLE CAUSE |
|---|---|
| Burning pain in the mid-back or lower back area. May come on after eating or drinking. | Duodenal or stomach ulcer |
| Back pain with pain around lower ribs. Possible pain in tip of one shoulder. Cough, fever, pain on breathing in. | Lung infection, possibly pneumonia or pleurisy |
| Back pain accompanied by severe chest pain which may spread to jaw or down one arm. Possible shortness of breath, dizziness, nausea, palpitations, feeling faint, feeling cold. | Heart attack |
| Women: dull, generalized low back pain. | Menstrual pain or premenstrual tension (PMT) |
| Women: back pain with stomach pain, vaginal discharge and/or pain during sexual intercourse. | Infections of the womb and/or Fallopian tubes |
| Women: dull, dragging pain in the lower back. | Prolapsed womb |

NOTE: The information and recommendations given in this book are not intended to be a substitute for medical advice. Consult your doctor before acting on any of the suggestions in this book.

CHAPTER THREE

# Sports and your back

*K*eeping fit is one of the best ways to prevent back problems *from happening in the first place or, if you have already experienced back pain, of ensuring that it does not return.*

Regular exercise helps to keep the muscles in your back strong and the joints flexible, thus preventing it from being damaged by the stresses of everyday life. An additional benefit is that if you do injure your back, recovery will take place more quickly if you are fit and healthy.

If you are a back-pain sufferer it is tempting to blame your condition on some physical problem that will be fixed as soon as you find the right treatment for it. In many cases this is true. Pain caused by joint problems and damaged discs can be relieved by the right therapy. But for many the truth may be that their backs hurt because their busy, sedentary lives have resulted in their becoming overweight and out of shape: their muscles are too weak and they are too heavy.

When you bend, lift, twist and carry, your back and stomach muscles have to work at full stretch against your body weight and the pull of gravity. If your muscles are weak from disuse they are much more likely to be over-stressed when suddenly called upon to perform a little harder, when you have to carry heavy objects, lift things in and out of the car or do some gardening, for example. Being overweight may increase this stress.

*Jogging is excellent cardiovascular exercise, but its pounding action, particularly on hard pavements, can exacerbate back pain.*

## A simple solution

One way of reducing back pain is to get more exercise. Even if your back pain is due to a structural problem and is alleviated by the right therapy, do not just give a sigh of relief and forget about it. Ask yourself why the problem occurred in the first place. Was it due to an accident or similar event outside your control or was it because you were out of shape when you tried to lift the end of the sofa? If it was the latter, getting fit will help prevent it from happening again. Most experts agree that once you have had one bout of back pain you are much more likely to suffer another in the future. They also agree that regular exercise is the best way of preventing recurrences.

Obviously, if you are still in pain it is not sensible to take up running or swimming now. Although everyday activities such as walking should be resumed as soon as possible, even if it hurts, you must give your back time to recover before taking up any sporting activity. Once the acute pain has disappeared, there are a variety of exercises that can be performed at home every day that are invaluable for strengthening the back muscles.

These exercises will normally be given to you by a good physiotherapist or osteopath. You may well want to carry on doing these after you have recovered.

If you suffer from recurrent simple back pain or have just recovered from your first episode, then it is common sense that certain sports are not suitable ways of getting fit. These are contact or high-impact sports such as rugby, football and basketball. It is fine to play these when you are fit but if you want to strengthen your back rather than damage it, it would be advisable to get into shape doing something else.

## Walking

Many people do not think of walking as a sport but it is perhaps the best all-round exercise for anyone with back problems. Brisk walking for 30 minutes or so four or five times a week exercises the whole body and improves muscle tone and cardiovascular fitness without the risk of injury associated with running. Walking does not require any special equipment, other than a sturdy and comfortable pair of shoes, and it can be built into your life relatively easily.

Most people, however busy, can find the time for a daily walk. If you commute to work perhaps it is possible to leave the car at home, walk to the station, travel in by train and then walk to the office at the other end. Alternatively, you could get off the bus a couple of stops early and walk the rest of the way. Perhaps there is time for a walk in your lunch hour or even your coffee break. You may find that the fresh air and exericse make you function better in the afternoon than you would if you had worked straight through.

Try to fit a regular walk into your routine at weekends. If the supermarket is within walking distance and you are not buying too much shopping, leave the car at home and walk there and back. Before you reach for the car keys, hop on the bus or take a taxi, stop and consider whether you could do your errand or journey on foot.

Walking briskly and swinging your arms will help you get the full benefit from your exercise. Remember to "walk tall" with your shoulders back and your head up. After a while you will find you are able to walk faster and further. Set yourself sensible goals and increase the distance gradually.

## Jogging

Although jogging is a hugely popular sport, anyone who has suffered past or recurrent bouts of back pain should approach it with caution. Jogging places considerable stresses on the knees, hips and spine. Normally the spine's ability to act as a shock absorber means that it can cope with the stresses – joggers are far more likely to damage leg and hip joints. But any spinal, joint or disc problems may be aggravated by jogging.

If you have never jogged before, begin with a series of brisk walks, and gradually build up the pace and distance before trying slow jogging. Try to lose any excess weight first, wear good-quality jogging or running shoes and always warm up and cool down properly. Take your time. If you are an experienced jogger who suffers from back pain, consult with your doctor before resuming jogging. ▷

## EXERCISE AND POSTURE

*Getting and keeping fit can help with back problems caused by poor posture – sitting, standing and walking badly. When your muscles are in good condition you tend to adopt a good posture naturally, partly because being fit makes it physically easier to do so, but also because you feel better about yourself and the shape of your body. Being fit also means that your back is stronger and more flexible and less likely to suffer injury when placed under strain, for example lifting heavy objects around the house. If injuries do occur, they are likely to be less severe if you are generally fit and in good shape, and you will also recover more quickly.*

# Sports and your back

*The twisting action involved in racquet sports can damage your back. It is important to get fit first if you want to take up sports such as tennis.*

▶ **Tennis and other racquet sports**

Racquet sports such as tennis, squash and badminton can pose problems for back-pain sufferers. These sports involve short bursts of running, sudden stops, turns, twisting and lots of bending and lunging to the side, all of which can put

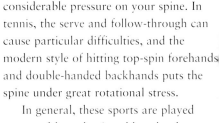

considerable pressure on your spine. In tennis, the serve and follow-through can cause particular difficulties, and the modern style of hitting top-spin forehands and double-handed backhands puts the spine under great rotational stress.

In general, these sports are played most safely and enjoyed best by those who are already fit. If you want to take up tennis, for example, get into shape with another form of exercise, such as walking, swimming or cycling, for a few months first. Then take a few tennis lessons in order to learn about footwork and how to hit the ball correctly. This will help you avoid injury while your game gradually improves. Lessons are a good idea even if you have played tennis before, at school for example, since they will help to make you aware of bad habits and will reinforce good technique.

Ensure that your racquet is the right weight for you. A tennis racquet that is too heavy will strain your back, shoulder and arm, while one that is too light will encourage "flicking" at the ball rather than proper strokes – with stressful and jarring results. Always wear the correct shoes for your sport. If you are playing tennis, do not try to make do with a pair of worn-out running shoes.

## Swimming

For people with simple back pain swimming is an excellent sport. It is good cardiovascular exercise and, because water is efficient at conducting heat away from the body, it is possible to exercise hard without overheating. As the water supports most of your body weight, swimming allows you to get fit without the risk of damage to muscles and joints associated with land-based sports. Front crawl, or freestyle, is preferable to

breaststroke if you suffer from neck pain or low back pain.

Many experts also recommend water therapy. This includes water aerobics and water walking. Water walking is wading briskly back and forth in the shallow end of a swimming pool, with the water at waist level or higher. Walking against the pressure of the water provides an excellent workout while the water supports you, reducing the pressure on your spine.

### Soccer

Although not in the same league as bone-crunching contact sports such as rugby and American football – neither of which should be played by back-pain sufferers – soccer nonetheless could further damage your injured back. Make sure that you get fit first before taking up this sport. ▷

*The natural buoyancy of the body is a great asset to back-pain sufferers, making water exercises excellent therapy.*

## CASE STUDY

*Sarah, a 49-year-old secretary with a large legal firm, had suffered several bouts of severe low back pain. She went to her doctor who examined her but could find nothing wrong. After some tests, she was pronounced fit and well.*

*Over the next couple of weeks Sarah's back pain gradually subsided. Then a colleague at work mentioned that she used to suffer back pain but that her back had been fine since she started swimming several nights a week. Sarah went to her local pool the next evening after work. She found that the "frog-kick" of the breaststroke jarred*

*her still-tender lower back and had to swim sidestroke. However, after 15 minutes in the pool her back felt wonderful and she resolved to swim three times a week.*

*Six months later, Sarah is still sticking to her resolution and her back pain has not returned. She is now fit enough to swim front crawl, or freestyle, for several lengths of the pool at a time and can do the breaststroke without hurting her back.*

CHAPTER THREE

# Sports and your back

### ▶ Cycling

Those who suffer from back pain may benefit from cycling as an exercise. As the cyclist's weight is taken by the bicycle, it is possible to exercise hard without over-stressing the joints. The bicycle should fit you and not the other way around. When

*If you decide to take up cycling, choose a touring or mountain-style bicycle rather than a racing type with drop handlebars. On a racing bike, the back tends to bend into a C-shape rather than its natural open S-shape.*

you buy a bicycle, have the seat and handlebar height adjusted to fit you. Wider, touring-style seats are generally more comfortable than the narrow, racing variety.

## Golf

The rotation and other stresses involved in a golf swing can put tremendous strain on the spine, even when performed by professionals. And, of course, most golfers do not have a perfect swing. Golfing injuries therefore account for a considerable amount of sports-related back pain. If you have recurrent back

## SPORTS AND YOUR BACK

| SPORT | SUITABILITY |
| --- | --- |
| AEROBICS | Not recommended for back-pain sufferers unless carried out in a swimming pool where the water will support your spine while you exercise. |
| AMERICAN FOOTBALL | Definitely not recommended if you have injured your back or suffer from recurrent back pain. |
| CYCLING | Recommended. Cycling is an excellent way of getting fit without placing excess stress on weight-bearing joints in the back and legs. Choose a touring/mountain bike as the head-down, bottom-up riding position needed on racing bikes bends the spine into a C-shape. When buying a bike get the seat/handlebar height adjusted to fit you. |
| GOLF | Not recommended. The movements involved in a golf swing can place severe stress on the spine, even when performed by a professional. However, if you already play and do not wish to give it up, have your game assessed by a professional, since poor technique may be causing your back problems. |
| JOGGING | Not recommended. If you want to jog spend several weeks increasing your fitness through brisk walking first and only then graduate to slow jogging. Lose excess weight before taking up jogging and always wear proper running shoes. If possible, jog on grass rather than pavements – perhaps around a local park. |

problems you should think carefully before taking up golf. If you already play and cannot bear the thought of not playing again, perhaps the best move – once you have recovered from your bout of back pain – is to have your game assessed by a professional golfer or a sports-medicine clinic so that any flaws in your technique can be corrected.

*Walking around the golf course is excellent non-stressful exercise, but a golf swing can place excess stress on your spine. Always warm up properly before you begin playing.*

**Find out more**

| | |
|---|---|
| *Skeletal system* | *12* |
| *Exercise* | *68* |
| *When back pain strikes* | *76* |

## SPORTS AND YOUR BACK

| SPORT | SUITABILITY |
|---|---|
| RUGBY | Definitely not recommended if you have injured your back or suffer from recurrent back pain. |
| SOCCER | Not recommended unless you are already fit. Get fit first with another less demanding form of exercise such as walking or cycling. |
| SWIMMING | Highly recommended. Swimming is perhaps the best all-round exercise for back-pain sufferers. It is excellent cardiovascular exercise and allows a great workout without putting weight on the joints. Avoid the breaststroke, which arches the back and can also jar the small of the back. |
| TENNIS AND OTHER RACQUET SPORTS | Not recommended unless you are already fit. Get fit first with another form of exercise, perhaps brisk walking or swimming. Take lessons and use a racquet that is the right weight for you. Always wear proper tennis/sports shoes in order to reduce jarring impacts from hard courts. |
| WALKING | Highly recommended. Walking is excellent all-round exercise for back-pain sufferers and can be built into your lifestyle. Walk briskly and gradually increase the distance. |
| WATER WALKING | Highly recommended as the water supports your spine. |

CHAPTER THREE

# Stretching exercises

*I*n *their desire to get fit, some people do themselves more harm than good. One of the most common reasons for minor sports injuries is a failure to warm up properly.*

Warming up, by gently stretching your muscles, is important because it prepares your body for the strenuous activities to come. It raises your heart rate, increasing blood circulation. This means your muscles are well supplied with blood and work more efficiently at the start of your exercise, making them less likely to be over-stressed and become injured.

Try these simple stretching exercises before you do any sport. Repeating them afterward will also help you to cool down, letting your muscles relax and return to normal gradually.

## Arm circling

1 *Stand upright and raise both arms sideways to shoulder height.*

2 *Rotate both arms quickly in large circles, five times forward and five times backward.*

## Backward stretch

1 *Stand with your feet slightly apart and your hands on your lower back.*

2 *Slowly bend backward while breathing in.*

3 *Straighten up slowly while breathing out. Repeat five times.*

## Forward stretch

1 *Stand with your feet slightly apart and hands by your sides.*

2 *Bend forward at the waist allowing your head, arms and hands to hang down. Sway from side to side for a few seconds.*

3 *Breathe in then, as you breathe out, allow your head to drop further down. Sway for a few seconds before slowly straightening up again. Repeat five times.*

## Hamstring stretch

1 *Stand with your feet about 60 cm (24 in) apart. Bend forward from the waist and clasp the back of your calves with your hands.*

2 *Let your head hang down. Hold for 10 seconds before straightening up. Repeat three to five times.*

**Note** *If you cannot reach your calves at first, place your hands on your shins. Practice will make you gradually more flexible and you will soon be able to reach your calves comfortably.*

## Thigh muscle stretch

1 *Stand up straight and step back as far as you can with your right foot. Place your right foot flat on the floor and facing forward.*

2 *Bend your left knee. Place your left hand on top of your left thigh and your right hand against your right thigh.*

3 *Move your weight forward over your left knee and hold for 5 seconds. Relax. Repeat on the other side of your body. Perform twice on each side.*

## Ankle stretch

1 *Stand upright. Raise your right foot off the floor, keeping your leg straight.*

2 *Slowly rotate your ankle to make small circles with your foot, five clockwise and five anticlockwise.*

3 *Lower your foot and repeat with your left foot.*

**Note** *You may find it easier to hold the back of a chair for balance.*

## Calf stretch

1 *Stand about 60 cm (24 in) away from and facing a wall.*

2 *Place your hands on the wall at shoulder height and lean against the wall keeping your arms and legs straight.*

3 *Keeping your feet flat on the floor, stretch your trunk to bring your pelvis close to the wall. Hold for 5 seconds. Repeat five times.*

# Your problem: its origin and solution

*B*ack pain has a bewildering variety of causes. The following
chart is intended as a quick-reference guide to some common
and not so common back problems, their possible origins and
solutions. It is not intended to be an aid to self-diagnosis, since if
you are suffering from any kind of back problem, you are
advised to see a doctor for assessment and possible treatment.
Afterward, you can undertake a course of complementary
therapy if you wish.

| PROBLEM | POSSIBLE ORIGIN | POSSIBLE SOLUTION |
|---|---|---|
| Pain and stiffness anywhere in the back. | Strained muscles due to postural stress. | • Short-term: massage, manipulation by osteopath/chiropractor.<br>• Long-term: investigate posture and/or environment for causes of stress.<br>• Alexander technique.<br>• Relaxation techniques. |
| Pain and stiffness in lower or mid-back. Perhaps also pain in buttocks, hips and thighs. | Strained or misaligned facet joint. | • Rest.<br>• Manipulation by osteopath/chiropractor/physiotherapist.<br>• Exercise after acute pain has gone. |
| Pain in the neck with restricted movement. | Strained or misaligned facet joint or possible disc problem. | • Manipulation by osteopath/chiropractor/physiotherapist.<br>• Exercise after acute pain has gone. |
| Pain in the neck with restricted movement hours or days after an accident. | Whiplash injury. | • See your doctor to rule out serious complications.<br>• Massage, manipulation by osteopath/chiropractor.<br>• Acupuncture. |
| Pain in the mid-back. | Strained or misaligned facet joint. | • Rest.<br>• Manipulation by osteopath/chiropractor/physiotherapist.<br>• Exercise after acute pain has gone. |
| Pain in the leg on bending the trunk forward. | Nerve root fibrosis. | • Special physiotherapy exercises. |

| PROBLEM | POSSIBLE ORIGIN | POSSIBLE SOLUTION |
|---|---|---|
| Acute pain in lower back with dull ache spreading over larger area. Pain normally confined to one side of the body. | Prolapsed disc. | • See your doctor before undertaking any course of complementary therapy.<br>• Rest.<br>• Manipulation by osteopath or chiropractor.<br>• Acupuncture. |
| Pain in lower back. Also pain in a buttock and down one leg. Possibly numbness and pins and needles. Pain may be worse in the back at first, then worse in the leg. | Misaligned or damaged facet joint or prolapsed disc – compression of nerve root causes leg symptoms. | • See your doctor before undertaking any course of complementary therapy.<br>• Rest.<br>• Manipulation by osteopath/ chiropractor/physiotherapist.<br>• Exercise after acute pain has gone. |
| Pain in upper back and down one arm, possibly into the hand. Possibly also pins and needles and numbness. | Misaligned or damaged facet joint or prolapsed disc Arm and hand symptoms caused by compression of a nerve. | • See your doctor before undertaking any course of complementary therapy.<br>• Rest.<br>• Manipulation by osteopath/ chiropractor/physiotherapist.<br>• Acupuncture. |
| Pain in buttock or groin. | Compressed nerve in the upper lumbar area of the spine.<br><br>Or<br><br>Referred pain from a "trigger point", perhaps in the lower back. | • See your doctor before undertaking any course of complementary therapy.<br>• Treatment for facet joint problems or prolapsed disc as above.<br>• Rest.<br>• Manipulation by osteopath/ chiropractor/physiotherapist.<br><br>• Massage.<br>• Manipulation by osteopath/chiropractor. |
| Sudden, severe back pain, often during sport or strenuous manual labour. | Avulsion. | • Rest.<br>• Do not attempt any action which causes the pain to return until your back has healed. |

NOTE: The information and recommendations given in this book are not intended to be a substitute for medical advice. If you are receiving treatment for any condition, consult your doctor before acting on any of the suggestions in this book.

# Your problem: its origin and solution

| PROBLEM | POSSIBLE ORIGIN | POSSIBLE SOLUTION |
|---|---|---|
| Severe, constant back pain in the elderly or frail. | Fracture due to osteoporosis. | • See your doctor. |
| Severe back pain with possible tingling or numbness in the legs. | Spondylolisthesis. | • See your doctor. |
| Pain, tingling and numbness in the legs. Symptoms made worse by standing erect and walking, relieved by sitting, squatting and bending forward. | Spinal stenosis in the lumbar region. Can be caused by a prolapsed disc, by joint changes due to osteoarthritis, or by the growth of osteophytes. | • See your doctor. • Lose weight to relieve symptoms. • In serious cases, surgery. |
| Pain in back or legs, with weakness, numbness or any loss of bladder or bowel sensation or control. | Compression of spinal cord or of the *cauda equina*. Can be caused by a prolapsed disc. | • Seek medical help without delay. |
| Back pain with fever and extreme tiredness. | Epidural abscess. | • See your doctor without delay – antibiotics may be needed. |
| Back pain with generalized aches and mild fever. | Influenza or fever. | • Rest. • Eat foods rich in vitamin C. • Herbal medicine. • Aromatherapy. • Homoeopathy. |
| Back pain with a stiff neck and fever. | Meningitis. | • Seek medical help without delay. |
| Pain in the lower tip of a shoulder blade, colicky stomach pain, possible fever and shaking. | Gallbladder inflammation or stones. | • See your doctor. • Dietary advice from a naturopath. • Herbal and Chinese medicine. • Homeopathy. |
| Intermittent low back pain with colicky stomach pain and nausea. | Kidney stones. | • See your doctor. • Dietary advice from a naturopath. • Herbal medicine. |

| PROBLEM | POSSIBLE ORIGIN | POSSIBLE SOLUTION |
| --- | --- | --- |
| Intermittent gnawing pain mainly in the mid-back area, pain in the top of the stomach, possible jaundice. | Pancreatitis. | • See your doctor. |
| Burning pain in the mid-back or lower back area. May come on after eating or drinking. | Duodenal or stomach ulcer. | • See your doctor. |
| Aching, painful muscles in the back and elsewhere in the body. | Food or drink allergy. | • Applied kinesiology.<br>• An elimination diet, but always take advice from a dietician or nutritionist. |
| Women<br>Dull, generalized low back pain. | Menstrual pain or pre-menstrual tension (PMT). | • See your doctor.<br>• Aromatherapy, massage<br>• Herbal and Chinese medicine.<br>• Homeopathy.<br>• Acupressure.<br>• Manipulation by osteopath.<br>• Yoga.<br>• Dietary advice from a naturopath.<br>• Relaxation techniques.<br>• Exercise. |
| Women<br>Back pain with stomach pain, vaginal discharge and/or pain during sexual intercourse. | Infection of the womb and/or fallopian tubes. | • See your doctor. |
| Women<br>Dull, dragging pain in the lower back. | Prolapsed womb. | • See your doctor. |

NOTE The information and recommendations given in this book are not intended to be a substitute for medical advice. If you are receiving treatment for any condition, consult your doctor before acting on any of the suggestions in this book.

# 4

# YOUR TREATMENT

## OPTIONS

If you have not suffered from back pain before, probably the best place to start in seeking treatment is with a visit to your doctor, who should be able to allay your fears that the pain might be a serious problem. Regular sufferers may want to proceed straight to their osteopath or chiropractor.

Many people find that mixing and matching conventional and complementary therapies is the most effective way of dealing with their pain. This chapter outlines the various treatment options available to help you make an informed choice and find the treatment to suit you.

# When sudden back pain strikes

W*hen an episode of back pain strikes it is tempting to contact a health professional straight away. But there are some self-help measures you can take at home that may ease the immediate pain without the need to resort to specialist help.*

If back pain strikes suddenly or you feel that a problem is imminent, it is worth trying the following "first-aid" measures.

## Rest

For acute pain, lie down for a while. You can lie on a bed, providing it is not too soft, or on the floor on a sleeping bag or blankets. Being in a horizontal position places the least strain on your spine. There is no right or wrong way to lie. You can lie on your back, on your front or on your side – whichever is the least painful.

If your muscles are in spasm it may take you a while to ease yourself on to the bed or down on to the floor. Try sitting on the edge of the bed and then rolling slowly on to it, or use a support to help you get to the floor (left). Whether you are on the bed or the floor, do not prop yourself up on pillows. Try to make do with a single pillow to support your neck.

If you are lying on your back you may find that a rolled-up towel or a pillow in the small of your back and two or three pillows

*If you decide to lie on the floor, try holding on to a piece of furniture such as a kitchen chair for support (top). Slowly lower yourself on to your knees (middle). From there, ease yourself down until you are lying on your side and then gently turn on to your back (left). Reverse this procedure to get up again.*

under your knees make you more comfortable. If you are lying on your side, a pillow between your knees will support the upper leg and prevent it from flopping over forward, which can twist your spine. Lying in bed or on the floor will help relax muscles that are in spasm and you should find that the pain will ease slowly or disappear completely while you are in this position.

Although bed rest is comfortable and provides relief from back pain, it is not a good idea for more than a few days at most. There are two reasons for this. First, muscle strength diminishes surprisingly quickly if you lie in bed. Second, rest is not as effective as other treatments to which it has been compared for pain relief, rate of recovery and days lost from work. The answer is to keep yourself moving as much as possible. Once the severe pain has eased, change position frequently and try to get up and move around every half an hour or so.

## PAIN RELIEF

When the words "pain relief" are mentioned, many people think only of pills. But there are other ways of alleviating pain that can work alongside painkilling drugs.

## Painkillers

Do not be afraid to take painkillers during an acute episode of back pain. Drugs such as aspirin, paracetamol or one of the other over-the-counter preparations can ease your symptoms and so help break the vicious circle of muscle spasm and pain. Never exceed the maximum dose of a painkiller and if your acute pain continues for more than three or four days consult your doctor.

## Heat

Applying heat to the painful area of your back can often be helpful, especially for lower back pain. A hot water bottle in a cover or wrapped in a towel and placed at the small of your back while you are lying down or sitting can be soothing. Alternatively, use an electric heating pad. If you feel an attack of back pain coming on, try taking a hot shower to relax you before applying a hot water bottle or pad. Hot baths can also be soothing and relaxing for a painful back but during an episode of acute pain it may be difficult to lower yourself into the bath – and even more difficult to clamber out again.

**Find out more**

| | |
|---|---|
| *Meditation* | *102* |
| *Drugs* | *156* |

## RELAXATION AND BREATHING

*The ability to relax the body by controlling breathing is fundamental to most forms of Eastern meditation. Correct breathing while you are lying flat on your back in bed or on the floor will relax your body and help ease muscle spasms.*

*Breathing is such a basic function that few people give it much thought. There are, however, two ways of breathing. Normal, relaxed breathing chiefly employs the diaphragm, the powerful, dome-shaped muscle that separates the chest from the abdomen. As you breathe in, the diaphragm contracts, pushing your stomach down and enlarging the chest, causing the lungs to expand; air is drawn in to fill the space. As the diaphragm pushes down, the muscles in the front of the abdomen are pushed out. When you breathe out, the diaphragm relaxes, forcing air out of the lungs and allowing the front of the abdomen to flatten.*

*When you are stressed or emotionally upset, the way you breathe automatically changes. Instead of using the diaphragm, you use the muscles between your ribs to expand the chest and quickly suck in large amounts of air. This is a good emergency measure and supplies the body with the extra oxygen it needs to fight or flee. In some situations, however, this can lead to a stressful vicious circle that works like this: you are stressed, so you breathe quickly using your rib muscles; this means that you do not take in enough oxygen, so rush your next in breath, prompting faster breathing – and so on.*

*So, as you lie there, take the opportunity to examine your breathing and use it to help you relax. If you are breathing quickly using your chest muscles, try to change to normal, slow diaphragm breathing – breathing slowly through your nose. Each breath should follow the last naturally, your abdomen slowly rising and falling and your chest remaining nearly still.*

**BREATHING OUT**

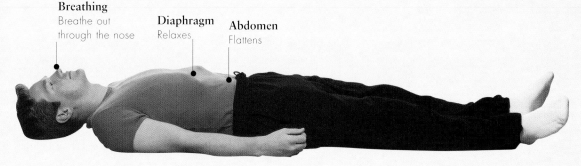

**Breathing**
Breathe out through the nose

**Diaphragm**
Relaxes

**Abdomen**
Flattens

# When sudden back pain strikes

*A simple massage can help to ease acute pain, but use only the gentler forms.*

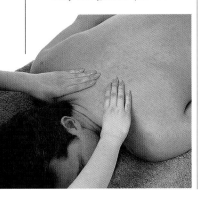

### ▶ Cold

Applying a cold pack to your injured back can also help ease the pain. You can buy special gel packs to put in the freezer from sports shops or pharmacies but filling a hot water bottle with crushed ice or using a packet of frozen peas works just as well. Remember that ice can burn, so never place the cold pack directly on to your skin – always wrap it in a cloth or tea towel first. Do not overdo this type of treatment – you can usually tell within 10 minutes if it is helping or not. If it does help, repeat the treatment after about 20 minutes.

### Hot and cold

Applying heat and cold alternately is a standard treatment for sports injuries. It helps reduce inflammation and swelling and promotes the circulation of blood around the injury. One way of doing this is to run a shower with the water as hot as you can bear it and direct this against the painful area of your back for about a minute. Then turn the shower to cold for another minute. Repeat this procedure for up to 10 minutes. Another way of applying hot and cold treatment is to soak two towels, one in hot water, the other in cold, and place them alternately

## SELF-HELP FIRST AID FOR SUDDEN BACK PAIN

| TYPE OF PAIN | FIRST-AID ACTION |
|---|---|
| LOWER BACK PAIN | • Lie flat on a bed or the floor. Place a small pillow under the small of your back and two or three pillows under your knees. Get up and move about every half an hour or so after acute pain has gone.<br>• Massage.<br>• Traction, horizontal or vertical.<br>• Application of heat or cold or both.<br>• Take a painkiller.<br>• Homeopathic remedies, especially *Arnica* and *Cal carb*. |
| LOWER BACK AND LEG PAIN | • Rest. As for lower back pain above.<br>• Massage.<br>• Traction, horizontal or vertical.<br>• Application of heat and cold.<br>• Take a painkiller.<br>• Homeopathic remedies, especially *Arnica* and *Cal carb*. |

*Horizontal traction may help acute lower back pain.*

against the sore part of your back. This is easiest if you lie on your stomach and enlist the help of someone else.

## Massage

Asking a partner, friend or member of the family to give a gentle back rub or massage can help to relax your muscles. There are many massage techniques that may alleviate the pain, although it is probably better to avoid some of the more vigorous forms, since these could create more tension and further pain. Make sure the room is warm, and that you are lying on a comfortable surface.

## Traction

There are two ways of applying simple traction at home to stretch the spine and relieve the pressure on the discs. To apply horizontal traction, lie on your back on the floor. Ask a partner or member of the family to lift your legs by the ankles, lean back slightly and gently swing your legs from side to side. To apply vertical traction, hang by your arms from a wide open door or other suitable (and strong) structure. Place a towel over the top of the door as near to the hinges as possible. Grip the top with your hands and slowly lift your feet off the ground.

**Find out more**

| | |
|---|---|
| *Self-administered therapies* | *84* |
| *Aromatherapy* | *92* |
| *Massage* | *116* |

## SELF-HELP FIRST AID FOR SUDDEN BACK PAIN

| TYPE OF PAIN | FIRST-AID ACTION |
|---|---|
| MID-BACK PAIN | • Rest. As for lower back pain (left).<br>• Massage.<br>• Vertical traction.<br>• Application of heat and cold.<br>• Take a painkiller.<br>• Homeopathic remedies, especially *Arnica, Lycopodium* and *Natrum muriaticum.* |
| SEVERE BACK PAIN ON ONE SIDE | • Rest. Lie on the affected side with a pillow between your knees to support the upper leg and prevent it falling forward.<br>• Application of heat and cold.<br>• Take a painkiller.<br>• Homeopathic remedies, especially *Arnica, Lycopodium* and *Mercurius vivus.* |
| NECK PAIN | • Rest. Use a soft pillow, with a piece of string tied round the middle.<br>• Application of heat and cold.<br>• Take a painkiller.<br>• Homeopathic remedies, especially *Arnica.* |
| NOTE | The information and recommendations given in this book are not intended to be a substitute for medical advice. Consult your doctor before acting on any of the suggestions in this book. |

CHAPTER FOUR

# Complementary therapies

Modern medicine is capable of amazing things: a course of pills can cure diseases that previously were fatal; surgeons can transplant organs, replace diseased joints and perform complicated keyhole surgery. Yet many people increasingly feel let down by medical science and are looking to alternative, or complementary, therapies, to safeguard their health.

If you have a specific medical problem, the chances are that modern medicine can fix it or at least knows how to fix it. It is with the less specific problems, the long-term or chronic conditions that often do not have a single, easily identifiable cause or solution that modern medicine may find itself in difficulties.

Doctors are often under pressure to see, diagnose and treat more patients in less time. This can leave people feeling abandoned by the medical profession when doctors say they can do nothing more for them and yet the problem has not been solved.

*Aromatherapy is one of the most popular complementary therapies, and many people have found it offers relief from their symptoms. An aromatherapy compress is easy to make and effective in easing simple back pain.*

### Another way

There has been a rapid growth of interest in all kinds of complementary therapies in recent years. There is an increasing realization that the relationship between therapist and sufferer is part of the healing process and that, in its race for technical excellence, modern medicine sometimes forgets this. As a result, it is easy for sufferers to feel that they are being treated as collections of symptoms rather than as individuals.

### A partnership for health

For many people, a major attraction of the complementary therapies is the empowerment they involve. Whereas the doctor–patient relationship usually entails the patient dutifully following a course of treatment, complementary therapies involve therapist and sufferer in a partnership of healing that explores all aspects of an individual's wellbeing.

Sufferers begin to understand how seemingly unrelated aspects of their life can affect their health in a negative way

*A close practitioner–patient relationship lies at the heart of many complementary therapies. You can learn how to take control over your own wellbeing.*

and how they can take positive action to improve the situation. Some complementary therapies, such as yoga and meditation, are suitable for use at home and are easily assimilated into daily life, helping to dispel the belief that healing is something done to you by someone "out there".

Another attraction of many of the complementary therapies is their lack of serious side effects. This is an important consideration for people suffering from chronic conditions such as back pain.

Finally, while conventional medicine can often do little to help people with problems such as back pain, research projects have shown that complementary therapies work. For example, a two-year study in the United Kingdom, published in the *British Medical Journal*, compared the effects of chiropractic and standard hospital out-patient treatment on 750 people with severe or chronic

back pain. Those treated by chiropractors reported greater improvements in their condition than those who did not receive this treatment.

## It's your choice

The aim of this book is not to advocate complementary therapies over conventional medical care. Its intention is to introduce you, as a back-pain sufferer, to the range of treatments – conventional and complementary – that is available. Many back-pain sufferers find that a mixture of therapies works best, hence the term "complementary" therapies.

It is important to remember that some causes of back pain, such as disc or nerve root problems, always need initial investigation and treatment by a medical doctor. However, even in these cases complementary therapies can play an invaluable role in helping to relieve symptoms and speed recovery.

# Choosing a complementary therapy

*Conventional medicine is beginning to accept alternative approaches, and your doctor may be able to refer you to a complementary therapist.*

O*nce you have decided to try complementary medicine, you may feel bewildered by the variety of therapies available. This book alone contains 26 different therapies, all of which have helped back-pain sufferers. So how do you decide which therapy may be right for you?*

At this stage it is useful to divide complementary therapies into three general groups: therapies that principally treat your body; those that treat your mind and emotions; and the so-called energy therapies. In practice, however, it is not this straightforward. Unlike conventional medicine; complementary therapies do not make a distinction between mind and body. Therefore the physical therapies have a psychological component, the psychological therapies have physical effects, and energy therapies straddle both groups.

## CHOOSING A THERAPY

| PROBLEM | THERAPY | PROBLEM | THERAPY |
|---|---|---|---|
| STRAINED AND ACHING MUSCLES (after sports or lifting incorrectly) | • Osteopathy or chiropractic<br>• Massage<br>• Aromatherapy | SCIATICA | • Osteopathy or chiropractic<br>• Acupuncture<br>• Acupressure<br>• Massage |
| MUSCULAR PAIN DUE TO NERVOUS TENSION | • Yoga<br>• T'ai chi<br>• Meditation<br>• Aromatherapy<br>• Self-hypnosis<br>• Psychotherapy and counselling<br>• Healing<br>• Massage | INJURED OR PROLAPSED DISC | • Osteopathy or chiropractic<br>• Acupuncture<br>• Acupressure<br>• Aromatherapy<br>• Homeopathy<br>• Massage |

Examples of physical therapies are: osteopathy, chiropractic, Alexander technique, aromatherapy, massage and yoga. Psychological therapies include meditation, psychotherapy and counselling. Energy therapies include acupuncture and homeopathy.

Many people feel happiest beginning with a physical complementary therapy as it seems closer to their normal experience. Nearly everyone has heard of physiotherapy and most people have experienced some form of massage. Of all the physical complementary therapies, research shows that osteopathy and chiropractic are the most popular.

Starting with either of these two therapies has another advantage. Today, osteopathy and chiropractic are largely accepted by the medical profession as effective treatments for back pain and

your doctor is likely to support your decision and may even be able to refer you to a suitable therapist.

After a few sessions you will know whether this is the right therapy for you. The osteopath or chiropractor may then suggest other therapies, such as yoga or classes in Alexander technique, if he or she thinks you would benefit from them.

Once your initial pain has eased, you can decide whether the problem is being solved or whether you wish to pursue other therapies. For example, although the osteopath or chiropractor may have identified poor posture as the probable cause of your back pain, you may begin to suspect that your stressed muscles are caused by underlying mental tension or anxieties. As a result, you may decide to try a therapy with a stronger psychological component.

**Find out more**

*Self-administered therapies 84*
*Finding a practitioner      146*

## CHOOSING A THERAPY

| PROBLEM | THERAPY | PROBLEM | THERAPY |
|---|---|---|---|
| ARM PAIN | • Osteopathy or chiropractic<br>• Acupuncture<br>• Acupressure<br>• Massage | WHIPLASH INJURY | • Osteopathy or chiropractic<br>• Acupuncture<br>• Massage<br>• Aromatherapy |
| STRAINED OR MISALIGNED FACET JOINT IN BACK OR NECK | • Osteopathy or chiropractic<br>• Acupuncture<br>• Acupressure<br>• Homeopathy<br>• Massage | MUSCLE PAIN FROM POSTURAL STRESS | • Osteopathy or chiropractic<br>• Massage<br>• Alexander technique<br>• Yoga<br>• T'ai chi |

NOTE The information and recommendations given in this book are not intended to be a substitute for medical advice. Consult your doctor before acting on any of the suggestions in this book.

# Self-administered therapies

*Complementary therapists believe that the basis of all healing is self-healing. To them, health care is an integral part of your life, not something that is done to you only when you become ill.*

In therapies such as yoga, t'ai chi, meditation and aromatherapy, the emphasis is on self-care. After learning the basics you can practise at home and make the therapy part of your everyday activities.

When you first visit an osteopath because of acute back pain, the osteopath will want to build up as complete a picture as possible of you and your individual circumstances. This will allow the practitioner to identify any other factors that may be causing your symptoms – factors of which you may not even be aware. The osteopath may then guide you toward other therapies that he or she feels will help prevent your back pain from returning in future.

These may include practitioner-administered therapies, such as acupuncture or Traditional Chinese Medicine, but the osteopath is also likely to suggest that you take positive steps to improve and safeguard your long-term wellbeing by learning and practising therapies such as yoga or t'ai chi at home. By doing this and making health care a natural part of your daily life, you will gradually be able to recognize the patterns of behaviour and tension that may have led to your pain in the first place. Having identified these patterns, you should be able to prevent them or at least deal with them in a more positive way.

# Yoga

**M**any people in the West used to think of yoga as an exotic practice from the Orient. Today, however, it is widely accepted and many enjoy its benefits.

The vision of yoga as something alien and Eastern dates from its introduction into the West toward the end of the 19th century. But now, a century later, it has gained wide acceptance and is recognized for its value to mind and body.

The word yoga means "yoke" or "union" in Sanskrit, the ancient language of India. The aim of yoga is to unite mind, body and spirit.

Yoga is not just an exotic keep-fit technique, although many people do initially take it up for its physical benefits. It is a complete philosophy that aims to bring the individual into harmony with the universe. In this respect, yoga is less a therapy than a way of life.

No one really knows how old yoga is but archaeological evidence suggests it probably orginated in India some 5,000 years ago. Although yoga can lead to "religious" experience, it is not a religion in itself. Its methods have been incorporated into Hinduism but they have also found their way into Buddhism and, to a lesser extent, into some mystical forms of Islam and Christianity.

*Many yoga postures look complicated at first, but with practice they can become part of your everyday routine.*

## TYPES OF YOGA

*The various types of yoga emphasize different approaches but all work toward the same goal. The most popular forms are:*
- *Hatha yoga emphasizes asanas and pranayama.*
- *Raja yoga emphasizes meditation.*
- *Ashtanga yoga uses meditation, asanas and pranayama.*
- *Kundalini yoga seeks to awaken latent, consciousness-changing energy that lies like a "coiled serpent" at the base of the spine.*
- *Tantra yoga employs asanas, pranayama, meditation and, in some forms, ritualized sexual intercourse.*

The literature of yoga is contained in a collection of texts, some of which are extremely ancient. The earliest written references to yoga appear in the Vedas, the oldest existing sacred Hindu literature dating from around 1550 BC.

### Scientific study
Yoga is one the most scientifically studied of the complementary therapies. Research shows that it can be beneficial for a vast range of medical problems, including back and neck pain.

The various posture exercises, the asanas, are the best-known aspect of yoga but they are just one of eight stages, or "limbs", of physical and mental training designed to achieve union. The asanas, in conjunction with breathing-control exercises, known as pranayama, are believed to unify and balance the muscular and skeletal systems before acting on a deeper level to harmonize the functioning of all the body's internal organs. Gradually they help to link mind, body and spirit and this eventually leads to the union of the individual consciousness with the universal truth – or God – a stage practitioners refer to as enlightenment.

## Spiritual or physical?

Yoga has helped many people in the West overcome all kinds of problems and to live fuller, more contented lives. For some it has also provided a gateway to religious or spiritual experiences. If the spiritual goals of yoga do not immediately appeal to you and you are simply looking for a way to ease your back pain, regular practice of the asanas and pranayama can still help you.

This is because the asanas work progressively to exercise and stretch every muscle in the body, including those not normally reached by traditional Western forms of keep-fit. If you perform yoga regularly, the muscles are thought to become more flexible and general suppleness increases. Underlying patterns of tension are worked out and the individual bones of the spine and the rest of the skeleton are gently realigned to their natural positions.

## A cleansing process

On a deeper level, the twisting, stretching, bending and then holding of postures involved in the asanas are believed to massage the body's internal organs, rinsing them in fresh, oxygen-carrying blood and draining them of old, oxygen-

**Find out more**

| | |
|---|---|
| *T'ai chi* | *96* |
| *Qigong* | *100* |
| *Meditation* | *102* |

depleted blood. The efficiency of blood circulation and of the respiratory and digestive systems are all improved. Meanwhile, the pranayama, or breathing-control exercises, help to unify mind and body and to control and focus the life-force. The overall effect is improved health and energy levels, and a calmer, clearer mind.

*With its emphasis on breathing, relaxation and body awareness, yoga can be an excellent therapy for back problems.*

## THE LIFE-FORCE, PRANA, QI, CHI OR KI

*The concept of the life-force is fundamental to most complementary therapies and it is of particular importance in the "energy" therapies, such as acupuncture and forms of healing.*

*This life-force, known as* prana *in India,* qi *or* chi *(pronounced "chee") in China and* ki *in Japan, is the basic energy of the universe. It creates physical matter and is the energy that gives us life. The therapies teach that humans and everything around them are merely the visible part of a vast invisible field of energy – a concept quite familiar to modern physicists.*

*The energy therapies work on the basis that ill-health results from imbalances in the flow of the life-force through the body. They aim to diagnose and correct these imbalances.*

# Yoga for your back

T*he benefits of yoga are well documented, but if you are suffering from, or recovering from, a bout of back pain, do not take up any form of yoga. The asanas can be difficult at first, even for someone who is perfectly healthy, so it is advisable to wait until you have recovered.*

## The mountain

1 *Stand upright and place your feet together, with ankles level, inner heels and big toes touching. Stretch your soles and toes on the floor. Balance your weight on the back and front of the feet, on the inner and outer side of each foot, and on the right and left foot.*

2 *Keeping upright, stretch up your legs and spine. With straight legs, pull up your front thigh muscles. Make sure your knees are facing forward. Keep your heels pressing down as you lift your ankles and shin bones.*

3 *Lengthen your waist upward and lift your rib cage. Create space in the top chest, taking the shoulders back. Keep the shoulders and arms relaxed, letting your hands hang naturally.*

4 *Comfortably lengthen your neck and balance your head above the legs, looking forward with relaxed face and eyes. Breathe evenly and smoothly, keeping your attention on the posture.*

## The cow's head

1 *Kneel with your feet flat on the floor behind you and sit on your heels. With an upright trunk, take your left arm behind your back, palm facing out, and bend your elbow so that your fingers point up your spine. Move your hand high up between your shoulder blades, still with the palm out, keeping your shoulders back. Stretch your right arm above your head.*

2 *Bend your right elbow and bring your hand down to clasp your left hand. The top elbow should point straight up and both sides of the chest should be evenly lifted.*

3 *Hold for 30 seconds or more, then release your hands. Repeat with the hand and arm positions reversed.*

## The shoulder stand

1 Lie on your back, with your head on the floor and your shoulders and upper body on folded blankets. Keep your arms close to your sides. Bend your knees and bring your feet in close to your body. Check that you are straight: legs in line with the trunk, positioned in the centre of the blanket, shoulders an equal distance from the edges.

2 Bring your bent legs up and over your stomach and raise your trunk and hips. To do this, press your arms down and swing your legs up. Bend your elbows and place your hands on your back.

3 If you can, bring your hips directly above your shoulders, and stretch your legs straight up. Use your hands to support your back in a vertical position, keeping your shoulders away from the ears, elbows down and chest open. Bring your chest toward your chin and keep your neck and face relaxed.

4 Continuing to stretch your trunk and legs up, hold the posture, breathing evenly. Usually the shoulder stand is followed by the plough (below), but you can come out of the pose by bending your knees and rolling back down, using your arms to control your descent.

## The plough

1 From the shoulder stand, take your toes to the floor. If your back is weak, keep your legs bent as you lower them. Straighten your legs and raise your hips, so that the front of your body remains extended as well as the back. (If you can't get your toes to the floor, support the front of your thighs on a chair, right.)

2 In the basic plough, the hands stay on the back. Lift your spine and extend your legs away from your trunk. Stay in the pose for 2–5 minutes without any strain in the head, neck or breathing.

3 To come down, let your back roll on to the floor. Allow your knees to bend and use your arms to control your descent, so that you do not have to land heavily on the lower back (if you have your shoulders on a high support, you can use extra padding under where your hips will lie).

# Yoga for your back

## Seated twist

**1** *Sit on your left foot, ankle flexed, with the inner left heel under your left buttock and the inner edge of the ball of your foot under the right buttock.*

**3** *Turn to the right, taking your left arm on to the outside of your right leg and your right hand flat on to the floor or a block or thick book behind you. Press your left arm against your leg to help you turn, keeping your right leg firm, shin upright. Hold for about 30 seconds. Repeat on the other side.*

**2** *Bend your right knee up and place your foot on the floor on the outside of your left thigh. Stretch up the trunk.*

## Reclining twist

**1** *Lie on your back and bend your knees up to your chest.*

**2** *Keeping the acute angle between thighs and trunk if you can, lower your bent legs all the way to the ground on your left. Your hips should turn so that you are lying on the outside of your left hip. Your right shoulder should stay down, but do not force it if it is painful or if it stops your legs from going to the floor. If your legs tend to lift or slide away, hold them with your left hand. Repeat on the other side.*

## The corpse

*1 Sit upright with your spine straight, arms by your sides and hands flat on the floor.*

*2 Lean back on your elbows and look down the length of your body to check that you are positioned symmetrically.*

*3 Lengthening the waist, lie back and rest your head on a folded blanket, so that your chin does not jut up. The neck and throat should be extended and soft.*

*4 Stretch your arms and legs and turn your upper arms out, so that the palms turn upward and your shoulders stay down, away from the ears; your arms should be placed a little away from the sides of your body. Relax your limbs completely. Your feet and legs will roll away from each other slightly, and your body should feel comfortable. Close your eyes softly, and relax your face, head and whole body.*

*5 Take a few deep gentle breaths, then let your breathing settle and become slow, quiet and even. There should be no strain in your breathing and no awkwardness in the position of your body. Hold for 5–15 minutes, breathing evenly and relaxing body and mind.*

*6 When you finish, do not stand up abruptly. Open your eyes without moving your gaze around, bend your knees, turn and lie on your side for a little. If you have been resting profoundly or for a long time, roll on to your other side and lie still before you get up.*

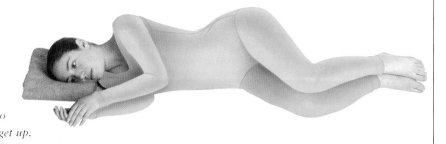

# Aromatherapy

*The use of essential oils from plants for healing and relaxation is known as aromatherapy. The art of using oils to enhance health and beauty is almost as old as humankind itself. The ancient Chinese, Egyptians, Phoenicians, Greeks and Romans all used oils as medicines and during religious ceremonies.*

*Manufacturers use a wide variety of plant components to make the essential oils used in aromatherapy.*

The term "aromatherapy" was coined by the French chemist René-Maurice Gattefossé in the 1920s. Gattefossé's conversion to the healing power of essential oils followed an accident in his laboratory. He burned his hand and instinctively plunged it into a nearby jar containing essential oil of lavender. The oil soothed the pain and, he thought, accelerated the healing process.

Manufacturers extract essential oils from different parts of a huge variety of plants by various methods, including distillation and expression (squeezing or pressing). Some oils, such as German chamomile, come from the flowering head of the plant; others, such as cloves, come from the buds. Yet others, ginger for example, come from the root, while citrus oils are extracted from the peel.

Essential oils are highly concentrated substances. They are, on average, 70 times more concentrated than the raw parts of the parent plant. This concentration means that they are used in tiny amounts and are always diluted with a much larger amount of a base, or carrier, oil. (The exceptions to this are lavender oil and tea tree oil, which can be applied directly to the skin.) Carrier oils are always vegetable oils. Typical carrier oils include wheatgerm oil, sweet almond oil, avocado oil, grapeseed oil and peach kernel oil.

Practitioners believe that essential oils contain the life-force of the plant and this is absorbed through the skin, or inhaled, to stimulate the body's tissues, promote healing and generally restore the balance between mind, body and spirit. The oils are believed to have painkilling, antiseptic and anti-inflammatory properties and to be able to improve the functioning of the immune system. Each essential oil has its own characteristic aroma and is believed to have healing properties. Some oils are soothing and relaxing; others are stimulating and invigorating.

## Essential oils and back pain

Many oils have more specific healing properties, and a number are particularly recommended for those suffering from back pain (see chart, right).

## Using essential oils

Like essential oils, carrier oils are held to have their own special characteristics and properties. Much of the art and fun of aromatherapy is matching the properties of the various oils, both essential and carrier, to achieve the result you want.

Of the commonly used carrier oils, sweet almond is believed to have a powerful healing effect on the skin. Use rosehip oil to treat scars and stretch marks. Practitioners recommend wheatgerm oil for its antioxidant properties. (Antioxidants are believed to neutralize the action of harmful free radicals in the body, and may offer protection against heart disease, in addition to boosting the immune system.) To obtain the best results, practitioners

## ESSENTIAL OILS FOR BACK PAIN

| | |
|---|---|
| BAY LAUREL | Rheumatic aches and pains |
| CLARY SAGE | Inflammation, aches and pains |
| EUCALYPTUS CITRIODORA | Arthritis and rheumatism |
| EUCALYPTUS GLOBULUS | Muscular aches and pains, rheumatic pains |
| EVERLASTING | Inflammation, arthritis and muscle pain |
| GERMAN CHAMOMILE | Inflammation, arthritis and muscle pain |
| GINGER | Aching muscles, arthritis and rheumatism |
| LAVENDER | Muscle pain |
| MANUKA | Muscular pain, osteoarthritis and rheumatoid arthritis |
| MARJORAM | Low back pain due to muscular stiffness, arthritis |
| NIAOULI | Muscle aches |
| PEPPERMINT | Neuralgia and muscle pain |
| SCOTS PINE | Arthritis |
| THYME | Joint pain |

*For an aromatherapy massage, the essential oils must always be diluted in a carrier oil.*

recommend that you use no more than two or three essential and carrier oils together at any one time.

There are several ways in which you can benefit from the therapeutic qualities of essential oils. They can be massaged into the skin during an aromatherapy massage, applied to a compress to treat localized aches and pains, inhaled – either directly or indirectly via a diffuser or bowl of steam – or used in a bath. ▶

# Aromatherapy

### ▶ Having a massage

This is believed to be the most effective form of aromatherapy for back-pain sufferers, although all painful areas of the body can benefit from a relaxing aromatherapy massage.

To prepare oils for an aromatherapy massage, add between two and five drops of essential oil to 10 ml (2 teaspoons) of carrier oil and shake well. The proportion of essential oil in the blend should not exceed 3 percent. If more than one essential oil is used, the essential oils together should still only constitute 3 percent of the blend.

## Making a compress

A good way of relieving localized aches and pains is to apply an aromatherapy compress. Compresses can be used hot, to ease muscle spasm for example, or cold, when they can help reduce pain and swelling after minor injuries.

To prepare a compress, you need a clean handkerchief or other piece of cloth and a bowl of either hot or cold water. Choose your essential oil or oils, then soak the cloth in the water and wring it out. Add between six to eight drops of the essential oil or oils to the water. The oil will float on the surface. Fold the cloth into a shape that will cover the area you wish to treat and gently touch the cloth to the surface of the water in order to absorb the droplets of essential oil. Place the cloth over the affected part of your body.

Cover the compress with another piece of clean cloth and hold it in place with surgical tape or, if you are treating a sprained ankle or other part of a limb, hold the compress in place by wrapping it in clingfilm. Replace the compress with a fresh one every 12 hours or so.

## In the bath

An aromatherapy bath can be a wonderful way of relaxing and may help ease tense and aching muscles, as well as be relaxing for your mind. To prepare an aromatherapy bath, fill the tub with warm water and then add about six drops of an essential oil of your choice. Swish the water about gently to blend in the oil thoroughly. Do not add the essential oil while the bath is empty or while the water is still running – wait

*Inhaling the vapour from a diffuser can be an effective way to benefit from essential oils. Dilute a few drops of oil in water before lighting the candle.*

*Add essential oils to a bowl of steaming water for effective inhalation. A towel tent will intensify the beneficial effects.*

until the tub is full. Essential oils are volatile and will evaporate if they are combined with running water.

## Inhaling essential oils

The aroma of essential oils can be inhaled either directly or indirectly. To benefit directly, add a few drops of essential oil to a bowl of steaming hot water. Cover your head with a towel, bend forward over the bowl and inhale. This form of aromatherapy can be excellent for colds, respiratory problems and headaches due to blocked sinuses. Keep your eyes closed as you inhale the aroma – it is important never to get oils near your eyes. If oil gets into your eye by mistake, rinse with plenty of cold water.

To benefit indirectly, place a few drops of essential oil on to a pad of damp, absorbent cotton and place it on a warm radiator. The aroma will gradually fill the room. This can be stimulating or relaxing, depending upon your choice of oil. Alternatively, you could buy one of the various diffusers on the market. The simplest and most commonly used ones

have a well or saucer above a small candle, or night light, which acts as the source of heat. Fill the well with water and add a few drops of an essential oil before lighting the night light. Essential oils burn easily so make sure you remove the bottle of oil and the dropper away from the diffuser before lighting the candle. Never allow a diffuser to burn dry. You can also buy electrically powered diffusers as well as a variety of vaporizers.

## BE AWARE

- *Aromatherapy during pregnancy should only be carried out by a qualified therapist. You should not undertake aromatherapy during the first trimester and it should be avoided altogether in a pregnancy with complications.*
- *If you have a history of allergic skin reactions it is a good idea to have a skin test carried out by a suitably qualified practitioner, such as a clinical ecologist, before trying an essential oil.*
- *Essential oils should never be taken internally unless you are under the care of a practitioner or physician who specializes in this form of treatment.*

# T'ai chi

*The Chinese system of physical movement designed to harmonize the individual with the forces of nature is known as t'ai chi. Many people who practise t'ai chi believe it can lead, eventually, to spiritual enlightenment – the recognition of the true nature of the universe and the individual's place within it.*

On a practical level, doing t'ai chi regularly is believed to improve flexibility and fitness, speed recovery from injury and illness, help prevent further ill-health and relieve depression and other psychological symptoms.

T'ai chi is believed to have developed from qigong, which is itself based on the ancient Chinese philosophy of Taoism (also written Daoism). Taoism was founded on the teachings of the philosopher Lao-Tzu who is thought to have lived during the sixth century BC. It seeks to achieve practical and spiritual harmony with the universe through following the Tao, which translates as "the way".

Taoism teaches that all living things have their own path, their own personal Tao. It is only when you recognize your own Tao – literally find your way or purpose in life – that you become part of the great Tao or universal purpose. The most important symbol of the Tao is water, which always finds its own level. The Taoist aims to live as simply and effortlessly as water flows.

The graceful, slow, flowing movements of t'ai chi are designed to integrate the forces of yin and yang within the body, creating the balance that is essential for health and wellbeing, both physically and spiritually. As this balance is achieved the *chi* or life-force, is able to flow correctly through the body and the individual becomes harmonized with the universe and everything in it.

Legend has it that t'ai chi was founded by a Taoist priest called Chang San-feng after he dreamed of a never-ending battle between a huge cranelike bird and a snake. The two creatures were locked in mortal combat over a piece of food but neither could get the upper hand. He decided his dream symbolized the eternal contest between yin and yang.

No one is sure when Chang San-feng lived but many experts believe that t'ai chi developed when the principles of qigong were fused with the martial arts practised in China by Zen Buddhist monks, probably in the 13th century. Millions of people throughout China practise t'ai chi today for both its physical and psychological health benefits. It is also still used as the basis for a highly effective martial art.

*Yin and yang oppose and complement each other in a state of dynamic balance.*

## YIN AND YANG

*In order to set out on "the way" you must first recognize and balance the opposing forces of nature within you. These opposing forces are known as yin and yang. When they are balanced, the result is the t'ai chi. Chi (also spelt qi) is the universal life-force (the equivalent of* prana *in yoga), while* t'ai *means great. The concept of the life-force that flows through the universe and through all organic living matter is fundamental to many complementary therapies.*

*This state of balance – the t'ai chi, or great life-force – is represented symbolically by the t'ai chi t'u, more usually known as the yin and yang or "two fishes" symbol, because it looks like two fishes endlessly chasing each other's tails. The two fishes, one dark, the other light, represent yin and yang, respectively.*

## T'ai chi and your back

Back-pain sufferers often find that t'ai chi is an excellent therapy. Research shows that its slow, flowing movements provide the benefits of Western aerobic exercise but without the stresses and strains that frequently cause injury. Regular practice is said to help weight loss, improve flexibility and tone up the muscles and ligaments supporting the spine and the rest of the skeletal system, which helps to protect against the recurrence of back pain.

In t'ai chi the back is kept straight and the head is held high in all the movements, actively ensuring good posture. T'ai chi also promotes relaxation, contentment and a calm, clear mind. Those who practise t'ai chi regularly report that it helps them deal more easily with the stresses of everyday life.

## Moving meditation

T'ai chi is often described as moving meditation. Students learn a series of separate movements which are then strung together into a continuous sequence, or form. The movements in the form are always carried out in the same order, one movement naturally flowing from the previous one.

There are two versions of the form. The short form consists of about 40 movements and takes, on average, about 8 minutes, while the long form has over 100 movements and can take more than 30 minutes. Like other types of meditation, the movements within the form are linked to controlled breathing. The time taken to complete the form varies from person to person. Some people are more comfortable with a slightly faster pace, while others prefer a slightly slower pace. ▶

*The stillness and ordered calm evident in this 16th-century Chinese painting of a meditating philosopher symbolize the Taoist teaching of oneness with the universe and everything in it.*

# T'ai chi

*2 Raise your arms slowly to chest level, turning your palms downward. Allow your fingers to open slightly.*

*3 Bring your arms across your chest. Push with your right leg to shift your weight on to your left foot.*

*1 Stand comfortably, feet facing forward, shoulder width apart. Keep your knees unlocked and relax your abdomen, arms and shoulders.*

## ▶ Practising t'ai chi

T'ai chi needs to be learned from an experienced teacher but the photographs here will at least give you some idea of how it is practised. Because of its emphasis on harmony with nature and the universe, t'ai chi forms are often performed out of doors. In China, people flock to the parks in cities to practise t'ai chi and other exercises in the early mornings, many arriving just after dawn.

There are several basic rules about posture and stance that are followed in all t'ai chi movements. The spine should be straight, the head upright and the shoulders relaxed – this fits well with the general rules on good posture.

According to the theory, the body's centre, or *dan tien*, is located just below the navel and inward toward the spine. Those learning t'ai chi are encouraged to visualize this as the centre of their weight and breathing and to think of all movements as starting from here. The elbows and knees are never locked straight but kept slightly flexed during all the movements.

When you first see t'ai chi being performed it seems as if the arms are by far the most active part of the body. When you try out the movements of t'ai chi for yourself you quickly learn that it is the legs, waist and trunk that work the hardest – your arms move freely and almost effortlessly.

4 *As you move to the left and your weight comes forward, allow your arms to uncross and move up. Keeping your elbows slightly bent, move your hands outward and away from each other until your arms are in line with your shoulders and your fingers are facing forward. Then slowly move your weight back on to your right leg, keeping your body upright.*

5 *Shift the whole of your weight on to your right foot, bending at the knee as you do so. Keep your back straight. While you are doing this, bring your hands back diagonally toward your waist so that the space between them gradually widens. Lift the toes of your left foot.*

6 *Keeping your torso upright, push with your right foot, so that you move up and forward, transferring your weight to your left foot so that the lower left leg moves into a more or less vertical position. At the same time, move your hands forward and up, until your hands are in line with your shoulders. Lift your fingers slightly so that your hands are at an angle of 45 degrees to the ground. Keep your elbows slightly bent. Then finish by coming to rest as you began, with your feet shoulder-width apart and your arms by your sides.*

## BREATHING AND T'AI CHI

*Correct breathing is extremely important in t'ai chi. Breathing in and out is timed to the movements. T'ai chi movements are classed as either gathering in or as projecting. Practitioners believe that the chi is moved more efficiently when you exhale. Breathing in occurs during gathering-in movements, while breathing out is timed to projecting movements. The aim is to breathe steadily and naturally during your t'ai chi practice and to synchronize your movements to this rhythm.*

# Qigong

*Based on the principles of Taoism, the ancient religion and philosophy of China, qigong focuses on learning how to feel and move energy within the body with the help of gentle, sometimes almost static, exercises.*

Qigong is generally held to be the precursor of t'ai chi and certainly predates it by many centuries. Archaeologists have uncovered evidence that qigong was being discussed and practised in China as long ago as 600 BC. By the 16th century AD, qigong was closely associated with Taoist and Buddhist monasteries in China – the fusion of its principles with the martial arts at the time being practised by the monks is believed have resulted in the development of t'ai chi.

Qigong is still practised daily by millions of people in China. Despite its deceptively simple-looking exercises, qigong is complex and it can be difficult to find out how to begin with this therapy. Its thousands of years of history have encouraged the development of different schools, or approaches.

Qigong exercises direct the practitioner's attention to the movement of *qi*, or the life force, within the body in order to build up what the Chinese refer to as great "inner strength" in a flexible, relaxed body. This contrasts with the "external strength", in the form of well-toned muscles, developed by practitioners of martial arts such as karate.

## Qigong and your back

Unlike its more active cousin, t'ai chi, qigong is unlikely to physically strengthen weak or damaged muscles and ligaments, but it can benefit back-pain sufferers in other less direct, but often just as effective, ways.

As back pain can be a result of chronic muscular tension, qigong is an excellent method of combating stress and

*1 The soles of your feet should be well in contact with the floor, not collapsing inward or outward.*

*2 Keeping your chin tucked in, raise your hands, with palms facing toward you, to shoulder height.*

promoting both mental and physical relaxation. Regular practice can help prevent a recurrence of the back problem. Back pain can also be a symptom of illness or chronic disorder elsewhere in the body. Qigong is reputed to have a beneficial effect on various chronic conditions, especially those that involve dysfunction of the immune system.

## Practising qigong

There is one principal difference between the Eastern movement and balance therapies, such as qigong and t'ai chi, and the Western "keep-fit" approach to exercise. The Eastern therapies are concerned with generating and conserving energy, while the Western approach concentrates on using up energy and

shedding it as burned calories, as well as on strengthening muscles.

As with t'ai chi, qigong aims to avoid placing stress on the muscles and joints. However, unlike the flowing sequence of movements in t'ai chi, qigong practice can involve standing still for considerable periods of time, concentrating on the movement of *qi* throughout the body. Other qigong movements involve gentle stretching or bending exercises that aim to promote the flow of *qi* to and through specific parts of the body.

The relative simplicity of some qigong postures means that it is possible to teach yourself the basics from a book. However, to benefit properly from both the physical and mental aspects of the discipline, it is important to find a good teacher.

3 *As you breathe in, turn your palms outward and raise your hands to just above eye level.*

4 *Maintaining your gaze straight ahead, bring your arms outward, so the palms face down.*

5 *Breathing out, bring your hands toward each other at chest level, with the palms facing each other.*

# Meditation

*F*or thousands of years, meditation in various forms has been used as a path to spiritual enlightenment, but today it is also practised by millions of people worldwide for a more pragmatic reason – their health.

Regular meditation promotes feelings of wellbeing, mental clarity, lightness and peace. Medical research has confirmed that meditation can improve mental and physical health. It induces a state of deep relaxation, which many experts believe is superior to sleep in its ability to refresh and heal mind and body.

During meditation the heart rate and rate of breathing can both decrease, and brain activity may alter to patterns only seen during very deep relaxation. Regular meditation may reduce high blood pressure and ease stress-related disorders. It can also have a beneficial effect on many other conditions, including chronic pain, muscular aches and pain, asthma, insomnia, heart disease and other circulatory problems. Those who practise meditation regularly report that their emotional stability improves and their powers of concentration greatly increase. Addictions and patterns of negative behaviour are more easily overcome.

## TRANSCENDENTAL MEDITATION

*The growth in popularity of meditation in the West owes much to the Indian guru Maharishi Mahesh Yogi. At the end of the 1950s he began teaching a new form of meditation which he called transcendental meditation, or TM, tailored to fit the needs of a busy, modern society. The Maharishi quickly built up a dedicated following and transcendental meditation soon became associated with the popular culture of the 1960s. Today, TM is still the most popular form of meditation in the West.*

*TM is rooted in Vedanta philosophy, which underpins the majority of the modern schools of Hinduism. Practitioners of TM repeat short words or phrases, known as mantras, in their heads to help them overcome conscious thought and reach a state of deep consciousness, sometimes referred to as "thought-free awareness or restful alertness. This state is believed to transcend thought – hence transcendental meditation – allowing individuals direct access to their energy and creative centre.*

*Practitioners choose their mantras carefully to fit their personality and occupation and most meditate twice a day for 15–20 minutes at a time. Most of the research into the effects of meditation on mental and physical health has involved practitioners of TM.*

# BRAIN AND MUSCLE ACTIVITY

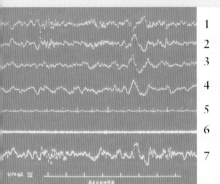

1
2
3
4
5
6
7

*During meditation, patterns of brain and muscle activity resemble those of sleep.*
*1 Brain activity (electroencephalograms).*
*2 Brain activity (electroencephalograms).*
*3 Right eye movement.*
*4 Left eye movement.*
*5 Heart activity.*
*6 Muscular activity in the throat.*
*7 Muscular activity in the neck.*

## Meditation and back pain

If you are one of the many sufferers whose back pain is the result of muscular spasm, or strain or tension from mental stress, meditation could be the therapy for you. Even if your pain has a structural cause, regular meditation once the immediate physical problem is dealt with could still be of great benefit. Meditation may help to relax the patterns of muscular tension that may have contributed to the problem in the first place, helping to prevent a recurrence.

## Practising meditation

You can meditate in any sitting posture that is comfortable and allows your back to be held straight. The most important consideration is that the room should be warm but well ventilated, comfortable and free from noise, bright lights and other distractions. If the room has a telephone, unplug it.

Breathe through the nose rather than the mouth whenever possible. Breathe deeply, but gently, using the abdomen rather than the chest. Your abdomen should swell as you breathe in and flatten when you breathe out. When you breathe like this your chest should hardly move.

Most people find it helpful to concentrate on an object, such as the flame of a steadily burning candle, or to close their eyes and repeat a mantra of short words or a phrase in their heads. Some visualize a pleasant scene, perhaps a flowing river or a lake. Others focus on their regular, deep breathing. The key is to find the thing that works for you.

The aim of meditation is to free the mind from conscious control, to allow it to become empty, to just "be" rather than to be thinking about something. You have to learn to let go of conscious thoughts and anxieties and allow the deeper, calmer part of you to emerge. Inevitably your mind will wander. Accept this and do not become irritated by it. As soon as you are aware that this is happening, gently return your concentration to the meditation object you have chosen. With practice, you will gradually learn to correct these meanderings almost without thought and your stream of meditation will be uninterrupted by them.

Take your time and try not to become frustrated if you feel you are not making progress. If you force yourself, you are no longer meditating.

# Hypnosis and self-hypnosis

Hypnotism's ability to reach and make connections in the individual's subconscious makes it a powerful tool for healing. In recent years the benefits of applied hypnosis, in the form of hypnotherapy, have begun to be recognized. However, the history of hypnotism means that many people still regard it with a mixture of fear and scepticism.

*Once you have learned the technique of self-hypnosis, regular practice can be a great help in controlling your back pain.*

Throughout history there have been healers reputedly able to cure the sick after placing them in a state resembling sleep. Modern medicine's interest in the potential healing powers of hypnosis began in the 18th century as a result the work of the Austrian physician Franz Anton Mesmer. Mesmer, who lived and worked in Paris, pioneered the uses of both hypnotism and psychoanalysis (a technique elaborated by Sigmund Freud more than 100 years later) in medicine.

Mesmer believed it was possible to harness mental energy and developed rituals around his treatments that hypnotized, or "mesmerized", his patients. His ideas were fashionable for a time but he was later denounced as a fraud by the French Academy of Medicine.

In the 1840s, however, Mesmer's work was taken up by Scottish physician James Braid. Braid showed that a trance could be induced easily and that, while in this condition, individuals could not be forced to act against their will. As a result, the medical profession began to take a serious interest in hypnotism and for many years, until the introduction of safe anaesthetics, it was used to reduce pain during surgery.

At the end of the 19th century Freud used hypnotism to help patients remember traumas in their childhood but then abandoned the technique in favour of psychoanalysis. Hypnotism fell into decline until the 1950s, but in 1958 the American Medical Association approved hypnotism as a useful medical tool.

Since then, hypnotherapy has been used to treat a great number of physical and psychological problems, including chronic pain, migraine, headaches, muscle tension, anxiety states, stress-related conditions, depression, addictions and phobias. Dentists often use hypnotherapy to overcome a patient's fear of pain, while obstetricians frequently employ the technique to reduce pain during childbirth.

## Hypnotherapy in practice

A hypnotic trance is a state between waking and sleeping. In this state you are aware of everything going on around you but feel completely detached from it. However, you are able to speak and to end the trance if you wish to.

For years scientists have tried to explain how hypnotherapy works. Many experts now believe that hypnosis puts the two sides of the brain – the left, which tends to deal with language and logic, and the right, which handles emotions and symbolism – in closer communication with each other. This allows connections between behaviour and its underlying causes to be identified and understood.

Research has shown that during a hypnotic trance the body relaxes deeply and that there are beneficial changes in heart rate, breathing and blood pressure similar to those seen during meditation.

Although in skilled hands hypnosis is a very safe technique, it can be dangerous if mishandled, so it is important to consult a qualified practitioner, preferably one with training in clinical psychology, or a therapist who is also a medical doctor or a dentist. Most people can be hypnotized easily and practitioners use a variety of standard techniques.

## A hypnotherapy session

The therapy will take place in the practitioner's office, which usually has subdued lighting and comfortable furniture. When you are sitting or reclining comfortably, the therapist will carefully explain what is involved in the process. You should feel relaxed, calm and, above all, safe. (If, for any reason, you do not feel at ease with the therapist, do not feel awkward about terminating the session at this stage.)

The therapist will attempt to relax you further by asking you to imagine you are drifting or sinking into comfort or by describing a beautiful, peaceful scene to you. As you relax, your eyelids will begin to feel heavy and your eyes will close. You are aware but detached.

Once you are in a light trance, the therapist can start to investigate the causes of your particular condition or problem and, once they are identified, can suggest solutions to you. There is a widespread, but unfounded, fear that once under the "spell" of a hypnotist individuals can be made to behave in uncharacteristic ways. In this condition you are open to suggestion but cannot be made to accept or do anything you would not normally wish to.

## The hypnotic state

If hypnotism appeals to you as a therapy, you should visit a hypnotist. After a few sessions, however, you may also be taught self-hypnosis. This enables you to induce what is known as an auto-hypnotic state at home and remain in it for about 20 minutes at a time. The benefits in terms of deep relaxation and the effects on heart rate, blood pressure and breathing are the same whether you induce the state yourself or are hypnotized by a therapist. However, it is important that you are taught such techniques by a properly qualified practitioner.

*To enter into a hypnotic state, you may find it helpful to imagine yourself in a tranquil setting.*

# Practitioner-administered therapies

*In complementary medicine you are always in charge of your own healing and the focus is on you rather than the healer. There is no firm divide between self-care and practitioner-administered care.*

Practised regularly as part of a generally healthy lifestyle, the self-care therapies can help to keep you fit and well and may prevent recurrences of your back pain. However, there will be times when you need or want the skilled care of a practitioner.

A complementary therapist adapts the treatment to suit your individual circumstances, with the intention of encouraging your body to heal itself in the best way possible. This approach is very different from the conventional medical principle of treating physical symptoms in isolation, and using the same remedy for everyone, regardless of physical, mental and emotional differences. Truly holistic therapists treat the individual as a complex mixture of interacting influences, rather than just representative of a recognized problem requiring an established solution.

Consulting a practitioner of complementary medicine is likely to be much less formal than visiting your family doctor. Many therapists have a relaxed dress code and practise in a room at home. The emphasis on relaxation, warmth and security means that you may wind up looking forward to your sessions rather than viewing them as a necessary inconvenience.

# Acupressure and acupuncture

*B oth acupressure and acupuncture are an integral part of Traditional Chinese Medicine. Today in the West they are frequently practised separately from each other and from the other techniques of Chinese medicine.*

Believed to be one of the oldest healing traditions in the world, acupressure has been practised for at least 4,000 years. Along with acupuncture it is based on the concept of the manipulation of energy pathways, or meridians.

Chinese medicine has a radically different understanding of how the human body works than Western science does. The Chinese believe that the functioning of the body is integrated with the functioning of the universe and that the same fundamental, life-giving energy, known as *qi* or *chi*, flows through both. However, the *qi* consists of two opposing energies, yin and yang, and these must be balanced within the body if good health is to be maintained. Yin, which represents the female life force, is traditionally believed to be passive and peaceful. Yang, the male force, is thought to be aggressive and confrontational.

According to Chinese medicine, *qi* flows through the body along 14 main channels, or meridians. The yin and yang energies are in a state of constant flux, ebbing and flowing in order to maintain balance and harmony. If these energies become imbalanced or if their flow is blocked in any way, the result can be ill-health and pain.

The meridians do not follow anatomical pathways as recognized by Western medical science but, according to Chinese medicine, each meridian has an effect on a specific organ or body system. Spread along the 14 meridians are more than 350 points at which it is possible to affect the flow of *qi*. In both acupressure and acupuncture these points are manipulated, either by pressure with the hands or by needles, to improve the balance and flow of *qi*.

### Acupressure

The practice of applying pressure to acupuncture points to treat ill-health and pain has existed for thousands of years. Chinese doctors use acupressure as part of their professional practice, and many people use it as a self-help technique as an alternative to acupuncture, which one cannot practice on oneself.

Acupressure practitioners locate the points that relate to the condition they are treating and apply gentle pressure using the tips of the fingers or thumb, the edge of a nail or sometimes small, round-ended wooden sticks. Occasionally special rollers, which can cover several points at

*By manipulating very fine needles inserted at precisely defined points, an acupuncturist hopes to restore the body to its natural state of harmony and wellbeing.*

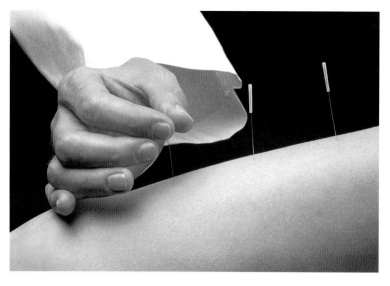

he same time, are used. Pressure, ometimes in the form of small rotations, s usually applied in the same direction as he qi flows along the meridian.

Acupressure can treat a wide variety of problems, including back pain, espiratory problems, headaches and onstipation. Unlike acupuncture, basic cupressure is relatively easy to learn and an be used as an effective self-help echnique.

## Acupuncture

Towards the end of the 17th century, a Dutch physician brought the art of cupuncture, which gets its name from *cus* (Latin for "needle"), and *punctura* Latin for "pricking"), to the West.

Practitioners insert very fine needles, many no thicker than a human hair, into the relevant acupuncture points on the meridians to regulate the flow of *qi* through the body. A skilled therapist can insert the needles quickly and skillfully, without causing the patient to bleed or feel any undue discomfort.

Chinese doctors have used acupuncture to treat specific illnesses and pain and as a preventive therapy since antiquity. Today, acupuncture is still widely used in China to treat a huge variety of health problems and is routinely used as a painkiller instead of a modern anaesthetic, even in major surgical operations. This popularity is increasingly reflected in the West.▶

## MOXIBUSTION

*Moxibustion is the ancient art of stimulating acupressure points with heat by burning a dried herb, usually mugwort (Artemisia vulgaris or moxa). Practitioners often use moxibustion for conditions such as low back pain, stiff neck and frozen shoulder.*

*Today, moxibustion is carried out in various ways. Moxa is processed into a woolly material which is made into small cones. These are then placed on the end of an inserted acupuncture needle and burned, gently warming the needle and the acupuncture point. This method can be particularly effective for arthritis and joint pain. Alternatively, the moxa cone is placed directly on to the skin over the appropriate acupuncture point. The tip of the cone is then lit but extinguished once heat is felt.*

*The safest form of moxibustion involves burning pre-rolled, cigarlike sticks of moxa and holding them close to, but not touching, the skin to warm an acupuncture point. Acupuncturists often teach this method to people with chronic conditions so they can use it safely as a self-help technique.*

# Acupressure and acupuncture

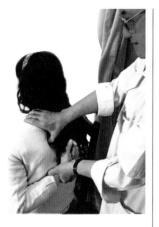

▶ In the West, acupuncture has steadily grown in popularity since the 1970s. It is now used to treat a variety of complaints, including back pain, arthritis, respiratory problems, headaches, migraines and digestive disturbances with many general practitioners recommending it in preference to drug treatments. Scientific research into the effects of acupuncture has shown that due to its relaxing nature, it is particularly beneficial for stress and anxiety-related disorders accompanied by muscle tension and pain. It has also been effective for treating addictions, for pain relief during labour and childbirth, and for controlling nausea after surgery.

Those who do not subscribe to the Chinese system of medicine admit that acupuncture works but are less sure about how. Many Western experts now believe that acupuncture stimulates the release of the body's own painkilling chemicals, the endorphins. *Qi*, the energy source acupuncture manipulates, cannot be scientifically explained, but it is held to be a form of electro-magnetic charge.

The needles are inserted into the acupuncture points at varying depths, normally a few millimetres. Each point has numerous indications associated with it. When treating back pain, for example, the practitioner may well include acupuncture points on the foot that lie on the urinary bladder meridian, which runs down the entire length of the back.

It is extremely rare to feel the needles being inserted and, if you do, it will just be a tiny pricking sensation, so you should not be apprehensive about pain. Depending on the position of the point, the needles are inserted to a depth of about 6-12 mm (0.25-0.5 inch).

## CASE HISTORY

*Jeremy, a 50-year-old accounts controller with a large construction firm, had suffered back pain on and off for most of his adult life. Usually, he just struggled through his bouts of back pain by taking painkillers and, eventually, the spasm would pass and life would return to normal.*

*Jeremy heard that the local doctor's surgery had arranged for an acupuncturist to practise at the clinic two days a week. One of the doctors said that acupuncture was supposed to be good for back pain.*

*At first Jeremy was not at all keen, being wary of needles. Finally, however, he agreed to go. At his first*

*session he was surprised at how long the therapist spent taking his medical history, questioning him about his symptoms and examining him. Jeremy found himself feeling thoroughly comfortable with the whole process and by the time treatment started his fear of the needles had been forgotten. He did not even realize the tiny needles had been inserted until the therapist told him.*

*After the first treatment, Jeremy's back felt much less tender and stiff and after several sessions he found that his problem had improved dramatically. A year later, Jeremy still goes back for the occasional acupuncture session. His back pain has not returned.*

# ACUPUNCTURE NEEDLES

*A typical acupuncture needle is made of stainless steel and, occasionally, silver or gold. It is about 2.5 cm (1 in) long, with the same length of grip. The needle is solid and has a rounded end, rather than the cutting edge of the modern hypodermic needle. The rounded end of the needle gently parts, rather than cuts, the flesh as it is inserted and the procedure is painless. Acupuncture needles are either disposable or are rigorously sterilized between individual treatments.*

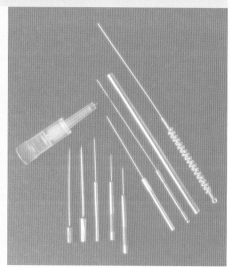

Sometimes the needles are left in place for a few minutes but usually they are gently manipulated by the practitioner to encourage the flow of *qi* at the site. Styles of manipulation vary greatly.

Normally the practitioner will manipulate the needles until he or she feels that *qi* arrives at the site. Some practitioners describe the arrival of *qi* as a gentle pulling at the point of the needle. As the patient you will normally experience a sensation of relaxation, comfort and warmth during the therapy. It is this feeling of mental as well as physical healing that is one of the strengths and attractions of acupuncture.

## Western styles of acupuncture

Various new forms of the therapy have been developed in the West, including electrical and laser stimulation of the acupuncture points. Machines have been designed that are, it is claimed, able to measure electrical currents along the meridians and to identify the best points for the treatment of specific conditions. These have become quite popular, especially in some European countries, and versions for self-help home use are also available. It is questionable if this is truly effective without the expertise of a trained therapist.

Many people who have experienced both the traditional and the Western forms of acupuncture feel that the introduction of technology into the process shows that, once again, Western medicine is missing the point. Healing is about the relationship between the healer and the healed, and technology, however sophisticated, frequently gets in the way of this.

## Other techniques

Auricular acupuncture is based on the theory that specific points on the ear correspond to specific internal organs of the body. Tiny metallic studs are pressed on the points and held in place with an adhesive bandage.

# Homœopathy

*Perhaps the most widely practised of all complementary therapies is homeopathy. Yet it remains one of the most controversial since, despite years of scientific investigation, no one can explain how it works.*

*Homeopathic remedies are made from plants, minerals and other natural substances. The active ingredients are dissolved to ever-increasing dilutions.*

The word "homeopathy" simply means treating like with like. It comes from the Greek words for "alike", *homoios*, and "suffering", *pathos*. The principle of homeopathy is that a substance that causes symptoms of a particular illness in a healthy person can be used to cure similar symptoms if they are caused by an illness. Homeopathy aims to help the body heal itself and prevent future illness.

This principle of treating like with like has a long and distinguished tradition in medicine. The ancient Greek "Father" of medicine, Hippocrates, was familiar with the concept, and it has long been used in Ayurvedic medicine, the natural medicine practised in India.

A German physician and chemist, Dr Samuel Hahnemann, developed the principle into a coherent therapy and published the first homeopathy textbook in 1810. Hahnemann's interest in the subject was aroused by quinine, the anti-malarial medicine extracted from the bark of the cinchona tree. He noticed that quinine given to a healthy person produced the same symptoms of fever and rigor (shaking) as malaria.

Hahnemann set about systematically testing the properties of over 4,000 substances. Experimenting mainly on himself, Hahnemann took high doses of each substance and recorded his reaction to it, a process known as proving. The basic ingredients of homeopathic remedies are still proved by being tested on healthy volunteers today.

Hahnemann then tested the substances in diluted form on patients. He selected patients who were suffering from a particular set of symptoms and gave them a substance which could cause similar symptoms in a healthy person. He observed that they got better. A person suffering from abdominal cramps, vomiting and diarrhoea, for example, may have been given *Nux vomica*, a substance extracted from the poison nut tree which, in large doses, caused the same symptoms. At the same time he realized

that finding out as much as possible about his patients before prescribing improved the success of his treatment.

Hahnemann noticed that patients often got worse before they got better and, in order to avoid this reaction, he began to experiment with steadily reducing the dose of the substances. This led to the development of the most controversial principle of homeopathy. Hahnemann found that steadily reducing the dose of active ingredients by increasing the dilution of substances and shaking the mixture at each stage increased the effectiveness of the remedy while reducing its side effects. This process, known as potentization, is used in the manufacture of homeopathic remedies today.

## Manufacturing remedies

Extracts from the natural ingredients, for example herbs, are dissolved in an alcohol solution and left to stand for anything up to a month. During this period the solution is shaken from time to time. Then the solution is strained off.

The strained solution is known as the mother tincture. This tincture is then systematically diluted to produce homeopathic remedies of various strengths. At each stage of dilution the solution is potentized by being shaken vigorously, a process known as succussion. The remedies are then made up into tiny pills – called pillules – granules or powders of the different strengths. ▶

## CASE HISTORY

*Niki, an artist in her late 20s, was poised for a big breakthrough in her career. After several years of struggling, she had been offered her first one-woman show at a prestigious downtown gallery.*

*With just 10 days to go before her show, disaster struck in the form of a bout of severe lower back pain. Niki spent half a day lying flat on her back with a hot water bottle and then rang her doctor. The clinic was very busy and the earliest appointment Niki could get was the following evening.*

*A friend recommended a homeopath who practised from home a few doors down the street. Niki dosed herself up with painkillers and went for a consultation. The homeopath spent nearly two hours talking to Niki and building up a detailed picture of her*

*symptoms, background, home environment, personality, ambitions – including how she felt about her forthcoming show – and even what foods she liked and disliked. The homeopath eventually prescribed Argentum nit, which is often recommended to overcome anxiety before major life events. She warned Niki that there was a chance she would feel a bit worse before getting better.*

*Niki took the remedy as instructed. The following day her back pain seemed worse, but she remembered the homeopath's warning and did not worry unduly. Over the next few days, however, the pain disappeared and Niki was able to throw herself wholeheartedly into the preparations for the show.*

CHAPTER FOUR

# Homeopathy

▶ Homeopaths believe that succussion causes the active ingredient to release its "energy" into the liquid in the solution. This, they maintain, alters the basic structure of the liquid, leaving an imprint, rather like a footprint, of the original active substance on each of its molecules. Therefore, even at dilutions at which there is no longer any physical trace of the original active ingredient, the liquid still retains an "energy memory" of it and this is sufficient for the remedy to be effective. Indeed, it is the highest dilutions that are the strongest remedies and it is this "less is more" effect that causes the most controversy about homeopathy in orthodox scientific circles.

The strengths of homeopathic remedies are classified as follows. A tenfold dilution is indicated by the symbol x, a hundredfold dilution by the symbol c and a thousandfold dilution by the symbol m. While over-the-counter homeopathic remedies are sold at dilutions of 6x, most homeopaths prescribe much stronger remedies at a thousandfold dilution.

*Thousands of remedies are listed in the* Materia Medica, *the result of Hahnemann's researches, published between 1811 and 1821, and the homeopath's source reference book.*

## A visit to a homeopath

Homeopathy operates on the fundamental principle that each person is an individual and needs personalized treatment. When prescribing, homeopaths take into account a person's personality, emotional and physical condition, likes and dislikes, as well as their symptoms. This is why a typical first homeopathic consultation often takes more than an hour and people with the same symptoms are often prescribed different remedies.

Homeopaths believe in the "laws of cure". These state that remedies start to work from the top of the body to the bottom, from the inside out and from major to minor organs and that symptoms clear in reverse order of their appearance. The "from the inside out" effect is known as the law of direction and means, for example, that as symptoms of asthma improve, a skin condition such as eczema may develop. Conventional medicine now recognizes a strong link between asthma and eczema: if one member of your family is asthmatic another has an increased risk of eczema or hayfever.

Homeopathic remedies are prescribed one at a time and, during a course of treatment, may be changed according to the way your symptoms progress. It is perfectly safe to take the remedies along with conventional medicines, although some drugs can reduce the effects of homeopathy. Alcohol, coffee, tobacco, strong mints, strong perfumes and aromatherapy oils, such as tea tree oil, can interfere with the efficacy of homeopathic remedies.

For the best results take a remedy on a "clean" tongue – do not eat, drink or brush your teeth for 15 minutes before or after taking it.

Many people use homeopathy as a self-help technique at home for simple ailments. But the holistic nature of homeopathy means that buying remedies to treat yourself is likely to be less successful than consulting a trained practitioner.

Today there are more than 3,000 homeopathic remedies and homeopathy can treat almost any health problem, although its effectiveness is said to depend on the individual. There are numerous remedies which may be prescribed for back pain. No two people are likely to be given the same remedy, even if they have similar sorts of back pain, so the list on this page can only be considered a general guide.

## HOMEOPATHIC REMEDIES RECOMMENDED FOR BACK PAIN

| | |
|---|---|
| ARNICA | Sprains and inflammation |
| APIS | Arthritis |
| BELLADONNA | Inflammatory arthritis |
| BRYONIA | Arthritis with sharp pains, backache |
| CAL CARB | Sprains and lower back pain |
| FERRUM PHOS | Rheumatic joints |
| HEPAR SULPH | Aching joints |
| LYCOPODIUM | Backache with stiffness, soreness |
| MERCURIUS VIVUS | Backache with burning, shooting pain in the lower back |
| NATRUM MUR | Simple back pain |
| RHUS TOX | Sharp pain, worse when moving |
| RUTA GRAV | Persistent backache, pain and stiffness from pulled muscles, tendon injuries |
| SEPIA | Backache, weakness in small of back |
| SULPHUR | Stiff joints, muscle cramp, lower back pain |
| URTICA | Rheumatic pain |

**Note** The information and recommendations given in this book are not intended to be a substitute for medical advice. Consult your doctor before acting on any of the suggestions in this book.

*Arnica*

*Belladonna*

*Ruta*

# Massage

*The benefits of massage have long been recognized. Around 2,400 years ago in ancient Greece the physician Hippocrates recommended, as the way to health, "a scented bath and an oiled massage every day" and "rubbing (to) bind a joint that is too loose, and loosen a joint that is too rigid".*

Massage as a structured therapy is thought to have originated in China and Mesopotamia more than 5,000 years ago. It continued to be an important part of conventional medical practice for hundreds of years and it was not until the rise of "scientific" treatments in the 19th century that it slipped out of the textbooks.

Most methods of massage used today stem from the work of Per Henrik Ling, a Swede, who came across Oriental forms of massage while visiting China in the 19th century. Ling brought these techniques to Europe and developed what is now known as Swedish massage. This system employs four basic techniques: effleurage or stroking, percussion or tapotement, petrissage or kneading, and frottage or friction. All these massage techniques are easy to learn and form the basis for most types of therapeutic massage.

A masseur will probably use a massage oil or aromatherapy oil to carry out the strokes smoothly, without pulling at your skin. Any pure vegetable oil or baby oil will be effective in lubricating the skin. ▶

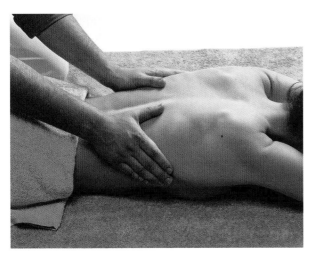

### Effleurage or stroking

*This warming and relaxing technique uses slow, stroking, rhythmic movements. The palms of the hands are used and the hands are kept close together. To apply firmer pressure, the fingertips and the base of the thumb can be used. For a more invigorating effect, this massage can be carried out more quickly.*

### Tapotement or percussion

*This, as its name suggests, is a brisk, stimulating massage. The sides of the hands are used with a light hacking, tapping or clapping action to chop and slap fleshy, muscular areas such as the buttocks, thighs and lower back. This sort of massage should not be used on bony areas or near broken veins.*

## MASSAGE VARIATIONS

**Find out more**

| | |
|---|---|
| Aromatherapy | 92 |
| Reflexology | 136 |
| Other bodywork | 140 |

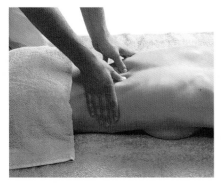

**Pressuring:** *The pads of the fingers or thumbs are used to apply deeper pressure to specific areas, such as around the shoulders. It can also be used in the lower back area but care must be taken to avoid direct pressure on the spine.*

**Knuckling:** *The hands are curled into loose fists and the middle section of the fingers is used in small, circular strokes. This sort of massage is often used on the shoulders, palms of the hands and the soles of the feet.*

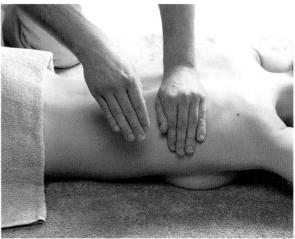

## Petrissage or kneading

*The fingers and thumbs are used to pick up and knead the skin and tissue. This technique uses more pressure than effleurage and is ideal for the shoulders, hips and thighs. It helps to relax tense muscles and boost circulation. It also improves elasticity and helps break down fatty tissue.*

## Frottage or friction

*This technique involves small, circular movements of the fingers, the heels of the hands or the pads of the thumbs applied over areas of muscle. The hands work through to the muscle below the surface without sliding over the skin. Carried out with moderate pressure, this technique releases muscle tension and improves circulation.*

# Massage

### ▶ Touching and your skin

One of the most natural, instinctive forms of human communication is touching. The skin, with its millions of tiny nerve endings, is the largest organ of the body. Touch develops early in life – it is the unborn child's principal way of investigating its surroundings. Research shows that babies and young children who are not touched and stroked are less likely to thrive.

Regular body massage can reduce anxiety, unlock tense and cramped muscles, ease stiff joints and generally results in increased vitality and a heightened sense of wellbeing. Massage as a therapy can be beneficial for a wide range of conditions and is excellent for back and neck pain. Other conditions that massage may help include muscle or joint pain or stiffness, anxiety and depression, stress-related disorders, headaches and migraine.

A massage can last for anything from a few minutes to half an hour or more. If you are giving a massage at home choose a quiet, warm room with subdued lighting. The person to be massaged, or receiver, should lie on a firm couch or on a mattress or blankets on the floor. You should wear comfortable, loose clothing that does not restrict your movements. Use large towels or bathrobes to cover areas of the receiver's body that are not being massaged. You can use oil – either a carrier oil or diluted essential oils – or talcum powder to reduce friction during the massage. If your hands are cold rub them together to warm them up before

## CASE HISTORY

Sharon, a young mother with two children, worked on the checkout in a large supermarket two days a week. The job was not difficult, she enjoyed the company of her colleagues and her mother enjoyed looking after her grandchildren for a couple of days a week.

Sharon usually worked two consecutive days. By the end of her second day, she often found that she had developed a nagging pain high up in her back, between the shoulder blades, which no amount of stretching seemed to relieve.

One day, one of her colleagues, Donna, confided that she wanted to train as an aromatherapist and that she had recently completed a weekend course in massage. Sharon mentioned her back pain and Donna jumped at the chance to practise her new skills.

The following evening, at the end of her

second work day, Sharon visited Donna's home for a massage. Donna gave Sharon a body massage and used essential oil of neroli, which is used for back pain and muscle aches. After the massage, Sharon's back pain had gone and she felt relaxed. Donna also suggested that the pain might be caused by Sharon hunching her shoulders as she sat at the checkout and advised Sharon to stand up and roll her shoulders for a few minutes every so often.

Sharon still works two days a week at the supermarket and she visits Donna, who has now qualified as an aromatherapist, for a massage about once a fortnight. Meanwhile, Sharon and her husband David have taught themselves basic massage from a book. Sharon still has the occasional bout of back pain but a 10-minute massage is normally enough to relieve any tension.

beginning. Keep your strokes rhythmic and flowing and try to merge one stroke into the next. If you are giving a full body massage, begin with the back before moving on to other areas.

## Shiatsu

Based on the same principles of *qi* and energy meridians as acupuncture and other forms of Traditional Chinese Medicine, shiatsu uses the techniques of both massage and acupressure.

A shiatsu practitioner makes a diagnosis in much the same way as a traditional Chinese doctor, by asking questions about your condition and your lifestyle and by studying your pulse and tongue. In addition, the practitioner may palpate your abdomen. Traditional therapists believe that each part of the abdomen relates to a specific organ or body system and that careful hands-on examination of the abdomen reveals any weakness in those areas.

The person being treated usually lies or sits on a mat on the floor. The treatment is carried out through the clothing so it is advisable to wear comfortable, loose clothes. The therapist aims to move and regulate the *qi* by pressing on acupuncture points with fingers, thumbs, knuckles, fists and even knees and feet.

One big difference between shiatsu and other forms of massage is that in shiatsu much of the pressure is applied in a stationary manner rather than accompanied by movement. Pressure may be applied for just a few seconds or for several minutes at a time. Treatments can last for more than an hour, with the practitioner also using body stretches to release muscular tension and gentle manipulation to realign the body and ease stiff joints.

Shiatsu can be effective for a variety of conditions, including back and neck pain, disorders of the digestive system, irritable bowel syndrome and headaches.

*A shiatsu practitioner works on the body's energy meridians and applies stretching techniques as well as manipulating joints.*

# Osteopathy

*Commonly recommended to treat back problems, osteopathy is gradually becoming accepted by mainstream medicine to such an extent that in some countries it is no longer considered an "alternative" therapy. In the United States, for example, osteopaths have the same professional status as medical doctors.*

The physical manipulation of the skeletal system to maintain and regain health is believed to have been practised first in ancient Egypt. Throughout history a great number of manipulative techniques were developed in China, Japan, India and North and South America.

Hippocrates, in ancient Greece, described manipulation of the spine, as did Galen, the Greek-born physician of ancient Rome. The Dark Ages and Middle Ages in Europe saw healers known as bone-setters, who combined massage, manipulation and herbal remedies to treat the sick. The ancient manipulative healing techniques continued to be practised by the Arab civilizations of the Middle East.

However, as with many other traditional therapies, manipulation was all but forgotten in the excitement surrounding the rise of modern, drug-based medicine in the 19th century. Then, in 1874, Andrew Taylor Still devised osteopathy and manipulation was given a new lease of life.

Born in Virginia in 1828, Still was a conventional physician for 20 years and served in the Union Army as a surgeon with the rank of major during the American Civil War. In 1864, a year before the end of the war, three of Still's children died in an epidemic of spinal meningitis. This tragedy rocked Still's faith in conventional medicine and set him on the path toward a new form of holistic therapy to which he would devote the rest of his life.

Still believed that the human body worked as a single, integrated unit and that to understand health and disease it was essential to consider the whole body, including the skeletal system, muscles, organs, blood circulation and other systems, as well as the mind and the emotions. He believed that a problem in any of these areas would affect the health of the total body. This approach is shared by most complementary therapies, regardless of their origin.

He was particularly interested in the musculoskeletal system, arguing that it was impossible to ignore a system that comprised 60 percent of the body's mass. He observed that joint problems in one

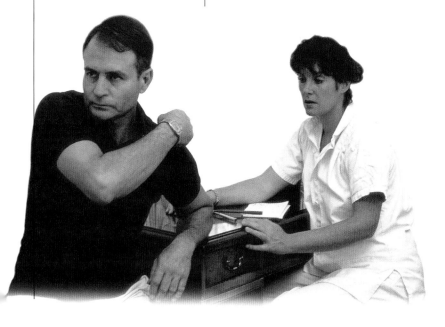

*At an initial consultation an osteopath will make a detailed evaluation of your condition and its possible causes.*

specific part of the body, while causing local symptoms, could also have an effect on health in more distant areas. Conversely, disease or dysfunction in distant areas could sometimes mimic the symptoms of a local joint problem.

On a more general level, Still thought that chronic muscular tension, caused by poor posture, injury or powerful emotions such as fear and anxiety, placed an unhealthy strain on the body as a whole, including the musculoskeletal system. He came to the conclusion that manipulation as part of a system of holistic health care could relieve pain, improve mobility and restore and maintain overall health.

Still called his new approach to health care osteopathy. But osteopathy as originally devised by Still was a far more global system of health care and

treatment than the strictly manipulative therapy practised by many osteopaths today. According to Still, osteopathy, of which manipulation was just one of many parts, could be used to treat all health problems and, initially, he practised his new approach in conjunction with the standard conventional medical care of his day. But he gradually became disillusioned with the crude and often lethally poisonous drugs available at the time and, by 1884, had rejected their use altogether.

In 1892 Still founded the American School of Osteopathy in Kirksville, Missouri. It had 18 students, including three women – remarkable for the time. In 1898, the school was one of the first medical establishments to install one of the newly invented X-ray machines as an aid to diagnosis. ▶

*Osteopathy focuses on the musculoskeletal system. It has proved to be very successful in the treatment of many back problems.*

# Osteopathy

▶ Students at Andrew Still's school of osteopathy followed the same medical training as conventional physicians but they also studied osteopathy. Today, in the United States, osteopaths are still medically trained doctors and there are now 15 osteopathic schools, 10 of which are publicly funded. Each year, an average of 1,600 students graduate as specialist osteopaths.

Outside the United States, particularly in the United Kingdom and Europe, osteopaths generally limit themselves to treating problems believed to result from damage to, or misalignment of, the bones and joints of the body.

## Osteopathy and your back

Surveys of people using complementary therapies in Europe and the United States show that back pain and pain from other joints in the body are by far the most common reasons for seeking help outside conventional medicine. In addition, surveys of user satisfaction with complementary therapies invariably put osteopathy and chiropractic top of the

---

### WARNING

*Osteopathy is a safe therapy that can be adapted for all ages and physical conditions. However, it should not be used if you suffer from any condition or disease that directly affects or weakens the bones or joints, such as rheumatoid arthritis, osteoporosis or bone cancer. Always consult your family doctor and discuss your medical history fully with the practitioner before undergoing any form of therapy.*

---

list. In fact, these therapies are now almost wholly embraced by conventional practitioners as the most effective treatments for back pain. If your back pain is due to a mechanical problem, then these two forms of treatment are probably the therapies of choice for you.

Osteopaths regard the body as an integrated unit and believe that a problem in any area can have a knock-on effect causing dysfunction and pain elsewhere. For example, they believe that if a misaligned vertebra puts pressure on nearby nerves, this can lead to dysfunction of various internal organs as well as the glands that produce the body's hormones. So, according to this view of the human body, once the misalignment in the spine is corrected the body is able to heal itself.

## Osteopathy in practice

When you first consult an osteopath the practitioner will make his or her diagnosis of the cause of your back pain in two different ways.

In common with most other complementary therapists, the osteopath will first want to build up as complete a picture as possible of you and your symptoms. You will be asked when the problem started, where exactly you feel pain, whether it is permanent or intermittent, and you will be asked to try to describe the pain. Osteopaths believe that it is important to take into consideration all aspects of your health and lifestyle before making a diagnosis.

The osteopath will then carefully examine not only the painful area of your back but also the rest of your body, to determine whether problems elsewhere are causing or contributing to your pain. You may be developing problems in areas ou would not normally associate with our back. The osteopath will check the movements of your joints and observe how your body responds to the normal demands of everyday life, such as sitting down, standing up and walking.

Once the diagnosis has been made, the osteopath will use various manipulative techniques to correct the problem. They can include flexing, stretching and massage. He or she may also suggest ways in which you can help yourself between consultations. Osteopathy is especially suitable for the treatment of back and neck pain, sciatica, sprains and strains and headaches.

## CRANIAL OSTEOPATHY

*Developed in the 1930s by William Sutherland, an osteopath in the US, cranial osteopathy is based on the theory that misalignment of the bones that make up the skull can affect the flow of the cerebrospinal fluid that bathes the brain and the spinal cord.*

*The bones that make up the skull are separate in babies in order that they can bear the pressures of birth. However, by the age of about two years they have fused together. Cranial osteopaths believe that, even in adulthood, these bones retain the potential for a tiny amount of movement and can become misaligned.*

*If the flow of cerebrospinal fluid is affected, this may lead to dysfunction elsewhere in your body. In such cases, cranial osteopaths use a light, gentle form of manipulation to realign the bones of the skull and restore a healthy flow of cerebrospinal fluid.*

*Cranial osteopathy is sometimes used when the part of the body that requires treatment is too painful for the patient to bear direct manipulation. It can also be used to treat various childhood problems, such as feeding problems in infants, colic, hyperactivity, learning difficulties and sleep problems.*

*In adults, cranial osteopathy is often used in the treatment of headaches.*

*Cranial osteopathy requires specialized training and is not included in the formal professional education of most osteopaths. While many conventional doctors now recognize the value of traditional osteopathic techniques, the medical profession has not extended this approval to cranial osteopathy, which is still dismissed by many doctors.*

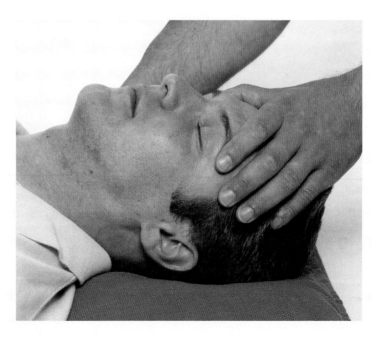

# Chiropractic

*T*he vast majority of the millions of people who consult a chiropractor each year do so because of chronic back or neck pain. Surveys of people using chiropractic show high levels of satisfaction, and a growing number of scientific studies have provided proof of the therapy's effectiveness in such cases.

Like osteopathy, chiropractic came out of the American Midwest in the 19th century and was largely the result of dissatisfaction with the conventional medical care of the day. Both therapies involve manipulation of the skeletal system, especially the spine.

However, of the two therapies, chiropractic has been viewed as the most controversial by the medical establishment for most of its history. A major reason for this is that, in the US at least, osteopaths, unlike chiropractors, are also medically trained doctors.

The term "chiropractic" derives from the ancient Greek for "manually effective". The therapy was founded in 1895 by a self-educated Canadian healer named Daniel David Palmer. Palmer, who moved to and practised in Iowa, established chiropractic on two basic principles: that spinal misalignment, which puts pressure on nearby nerves, is the cause of virtually all disease; and that spinal manipulation is the cure.

Palmer believed that by manipulating the spine to correct the problem it was possible to cure not only conditions such as sciatica but also a range of internal complaints such digestive disorders and even asthma. The subject of Palmer's first chiropractic manipulation was Harvey Lillard, the janitor of the building in which Palmer had his office. Lillard, who was deaf, was suffering a bout of severe back pain. Palmer manipulated his spine and Lillard's pain was cured – and so was

his deafness. At first Palmer thought he had accidentally discovered a cure for deafness but although chiropractic proved effective for all sorts of back and neck pain, Palmer never managed to cure another case of deafness.

Word about the new therapy spread rapidly, and by the turn of the century chiropractic had gained a considerable following. It was, however, viewed as controversial from the start, and hundreds of early practitioners were arrested for practising medicine without a licence. Palmer himself was jailed for a time in 1906 and the American medical establishment vociferously opposed the new therapy.

Although chiropractic had many proponents, suspicion and hostility continued throughout the 20th century. Matters finally came to a head as recently as 1990 when the United States Supreme Court upheld a lower court ruling that the American Medical Association was guilty of anti-trust law violations by engaging in a conspiracy to "contain and eliminate" chiropractic.

Today, chiropractic is the third largest independent health profession in the Western world after conventional medicine and dentistry. However, unlike osteopathy, physically chiropractic has stayed close to its roots and 52,000 of the world's 56,000 chiropractors practise in North America.

Most modern chiropractors would now find Palmer's original philosophy of

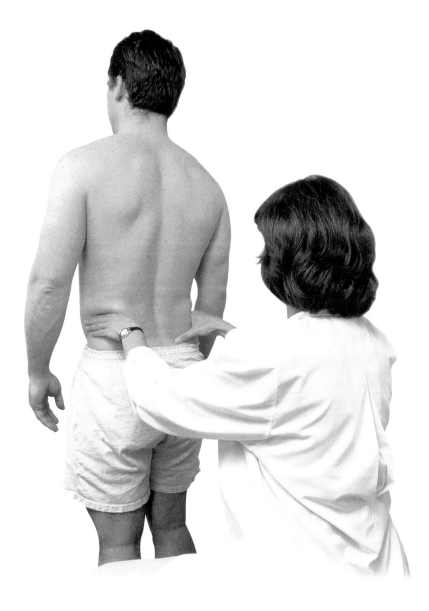

**Find out more**

| | |
|---|---|
| *Skeletal problems* | *40* |
| *Choosing a therapy* | *82* |
| *Osteopathy* | *120* |

*A chiropractor will examine your back for misaligned vertebrae, which may be the cause of back pain and other internal problems.*

one cause – one cure" too simplistic, but pinal manipulation does remain the ornerstone of the therapy. In fact, the mphasis placed on spinal manipulation y many chiropractors is probably the eason for the widespread belief that the herapy is only really useful for treating ack pain. In practice, however, hiropractors treat almost any mechanical roblem anywhere in the body.

Chiropractic is a holistic discipline nd shares many of the fundamental principles of natural healing that underpin all complementary therapies. In particular, the natural principles of chiropractic are that:

• All human beings share a natural healing potential or inner wisdom of the body

• The is the aim of the healing arts is to assist this potential

• The use of medical drugs to suppress symptoms can damage the body's ability to heal itself. ▶

# Chiropractic

▶ Chiropractors believe that overall health depends on the normal functioning of the nervous system – that pain and disease in any area of the body are the result of a malfunction of the nerves supplying that particular area. According to this theory, structural problems in and around the spine are the most common reason for such a malfunction.

In simple terms, if a nerve becomes compressed, by a misaligned facet joint for example, the flow of nerve impulses is disrupted, in much the same way as stepping on a hosepipe blocks the flow of water. This in turn leads to dysfunction in the organ or body system that the nerve supplies.

As well as causing nerve disruption, such structural problems can also have local mechanical effects as the resulting imbalance in the spine places nearby structures under strain, leading to muscle

## CASE HISTORY

Sean, a 39-year-old financial trader, was on a climbing holiday when he suddenly developed severe pain in his left knee. The knee swelled up and for the last three days of the holiday he hobbled around the hotel with it wrapped in an elastic bandage.

On his return home, Sean went to see his family doctor who examined the knee and referred him to an orthopaedic consultant. By the time of his appointment Sean's knee was still a little swollen but much better. The orthopaedic consultant examined the knee and told Sean that everything appeared normal. He thought it might be a slight cartilage problem but as it was getting better suggested they let nature take its course.

A week later, Sean got up from his chair at work and again experienced an intense pain in his knee. Once again, the problem gradually subsided. A week or so later a colleague told Sean that he was being treated for low back pain by a chiropractor. Sean did not know much about chiropractic at the time but he was interested enough to read up about it in a book on complementary therapies. According to the book, chiropractic could potentially treat all forms of skeletal and joint problems.

The next morning, Sean obtained the chiropractor's telephone number from his colleague and arranged an appointment. At the first consultation the chiropractor compiled a detailed picture of Sean and his health. He examined Sean's knee and the rest of his body and took several X-rays of his spine. The chiropractor diagnosed a spinal joint problem in Sean's lower back and said this was the cause of the knee problem. Sean was unconsciously compensating for the stiffness in his lower back by slightly altering the way he walked. This, in turn, placed excess weight and strain on his left knee which ached when under strain.

The chiropractor manipulated Sean's spine over several twice-weekly sessions and he has not suffered any knee problems since then.

pasm and pain. They may also have more distant effects. A structural problem in the lower back, for example, may place xcess strain on one or both knees, and in uch cases, knee problems rather than back pain are often the complaint that auses the sufferer to make an ppointment to see the chiropractor.

## A visit to a chiropractor

Like all complementary therapists, a hiropractor will spend a considerable ime talking to you and taking a detailed ersonal history when you arrive for your irst consultation. He or she may take X-ays of your spine to help with the iagnosis and to rule out any underlying iseases. The X-rays will probably be aken while your spine is under pressure – vhen you are sitting down or standing p – since the chiropractor believes that his will show how your discs and joints andle everyday loads.

Once a chiropractor has made a iagnosis, a number of different nanipulative techniques can be used to orrect the problem. For example, in the ase of a misaligned vertebra the reatment will include very precise djustments to bring it back into line.

If a joint is believed to have become oo stiff and lacks mobility, the hiropractor will use manipulation to radually increase its flexibility. Conversely, if it is too flexible, perhaps as result of slack or strained ligaments, the ractitioner will concentrate on freeing earby joints that may have become stiff nd fixed to compensate for the nisalignment and will suggest exercises to tabilize and strengthen the muscles round the loose joint in order to give it nore support.

## Warning

Chiropractic is a very safe therapy that can be adapted to suit all ages and physical conditions. However, you should not undergo chiropractic manipulation if you have any disease or condition that directly affects or weakens the bones, such as rheumatoid arthritis, osteoporosis or bone cancer. Always discuss fully your medical history with the practitioner before undergoing any form of therapy.

*Chiropractic techniques include pushing, pulling and levering muscle against bone.*

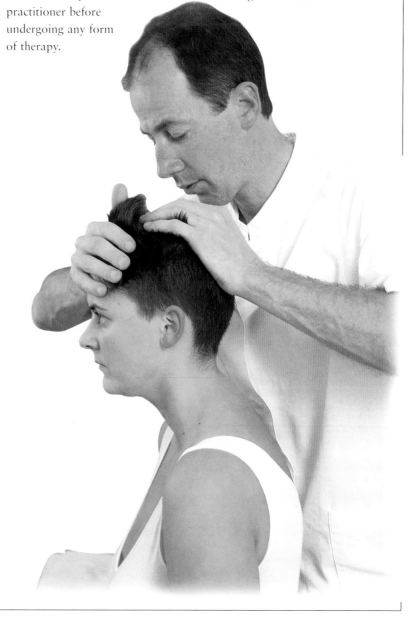

# Traditional Chinese Medicine

*For more than 4,000 years, traditional Chinese Medicine – acupuncture, moxibustion, acupressure, Chinese herbal medicine and cupping – has been practised in various forms. Today in China traditional medicine exists as a parallel health-care system alongside its modern Western counterpart.*

*Chinese herbal remedies are made up to formulas prescribed by practitioners to suit the individual needs of each patient.*

Much of Traditional Chinese Medicine is based on the *Yellow Emperor's Inner Classic*, a text written some time between 770 and 476 BC. The *Inner Classic* is divided into two books. The first, *Simple Questions*, deals with the fundamental theories, while the second, *Spiritual Axis*, concentrates on the techniques of acupuncture and moxibustion.

Traditional Chinese medicine was the only form practised in China until the collapse of the reigning Qing dynasty in 1911 and the founding of the first republic, when Western "scientific" medicine swept into China. The new rulers wanted modern medicine for a new modern China. Traditional medicine was legislated against and generally reviled by both nationalist and Marxist reformers in the first half of the 20th century.

But Traditional Chinese Medicine survived and, after the founding of the People's Republic in 1949, it was reinstated by the Communist government of Mao Zedong. Colleges of Chinese medicine were built and the concept of the "barefoot doctor" was born. These graduates from the new colleges practised deep in the rural hinterland of China, administering traditional medicine including remedies made from herbs they gathered and prepared themselves.

## The theory

Traditional Chinese Medicine is based on the concept of internal balance and harmony and on the relationship between the human body and its environment. When there is internal balance and harmony between the individual and the external environment there is good health. If this balance is disturbed, illness and disease can result.

Practitioners of Traditional Chinese Medicine believe in the concept of *qi* or *chi*, which is the fundamental energy of the universe. *Qi* flows through all living things, including human beings. In the human body, *qi* circulates through 14

main energy channels, or meridians, that are located just below the surface of the skin. These meridians do not follow any sort of anatomical routes as understood by Western doctors but each meridian is associated with a specific organ or body system. Along these meridians lie the acupuncture points, specific sites at which the *qi* can be manipulated and rebalanced to cure disease.

The *qi*, or life force, consists of two opposing forces, yin and yang. Yin and yang continually ebb and flow, are interdependent and must balance each other – much as night balances day and heat balances cold – if the body is to be in harmony with both itself and with the universe.

Yin is associated with coldness, darkness, night, earth and water. Yang is associated with heat, light, day, heaven and fire. Practitioners often describe an individual's personality and illness in terms of their yin and yang. A pale and shivering person who complained of fatigue, for example, would be diagnosed as suffering from an excess of yin, while someone flushed and sweating with feverlike symptoms would be judged to have an excess of yang. In each case treatment would aim to restore the yin/yang balance.

Practitioners of Traditional Chinese Medicine maintain that human beings have essence and spirit as well as *qi*. Together they are referred to as the three treasures. The essence is inherited from your parents and is the vital spark of life and the basis for all bodily functions. Essence is restored and maintained by food and rest. The spirit is the gift of heaven and is manifested in the intelligence and alertness that characterize human beings.

Another aspect of Traditional Chinese Medicine is the theory of five elements or phases: wood, fire, earth, metal and water. These elements must be in balance for good health to be maintained and will be taken into consideration during diagnosis and treatment. The elements are affected by factors such as the weather, diet and emotions.

## The practice

Although ultimately in Traditional Chinese Medicine all illness and disease is the result of a disturbance of the *qi*, the reason for this disturbance is seen as falling into three distinct categories: external causes, internal causes, and causes that are neither external nor internal.

External causes of disease are referred to as evils and include wind, cold, fire, damp, summer heat and dryness. Internal causes, known as affects, include joy, anger, anxiety, thought, sorrow, fear and fright. Causes that are neither external nor internal include poor diet, physical exhaustion, trauma, parasites and excessive sexual activity.

## Diagnosis

There are four different parts to diagnosis in Traditional Chinese Medicine: inspection, listening and smelling, inquiry and palpation.

Inspection is the practitioner's visual assessment of the patient. The practitioner observes the patient's walk, general bearing and demeanour and strength of spirit and notes the condition of the skin, hair, eyes and nails. The condition of a patient's spirit is believed to be particularly important and "good spirit" is considered to be an excellent sign, even in cases of serious illness. ▶

# Traditional Chinese Medicine

*Chinese remedies may be supplied as raw herbs or in powdered form. You prepare the raw herbs at home by boiling them in water and straining off the liquid to drink. The more convenient powders are prepared in much the same way as instant coffee.*

▶ During the inspection the practitioner will also look at the patient's tongue. In Traditional Chinese Medicine, the colour and condition of the tongue and its coating can supply important information about the health of the whole body.

Listening and smelling involve assessing the sound and quality of the voice and the noises of the body as well as the odour of the breath, the body and the excreta, especially urine. Any of these details can be useful indicators of imbalances within the body.

Inquiry involves taking an extremely detailed history of a patient's symptoms and general health. The practitioner may also ask about sleeping habits, diet, likes and dislikes, and general lifestyle, such as family, friends and work.

Palpation includes feeling various acupuncture points and examination of the pulse. This is a much more elaborate procedure than that carried out by Western doctors. The pulse is taken on the inside of each wrist using three fingers each time. Each pulse correlates with a specific major meridian and its linked organ. The quality of each pulse can give the practitioner valuable information about the state of the *qi* and conditions in different locations of the body.

## Herbal treatment

The most important surviving text on traditional Chinese herbalism was written in the 16th century by the physician Li Shih-Chen. It lists 2,000 herbs and a total of 10,000 remedies. More common today is the *Encyclopedia of Traditional Chinese Medicinal Substances* contains 5,767 entries.

Most of the "raw" ingredients of Chinese herbal medicines are plants but some come from mineral or animal sources. Chinese medicine tends to prescribe a combination of different herbs, carefully tailored to the individual patient. The herbs are chosen not only for their effects on your specific condition or disease but also for their compatibility with each other and with what your practitioner has learned of your constitution. The ingredients of this cocktail of herbs may be altered as treatment progresses and your condition begins to improve.

Different herbs are classified as cold, cool, warm, hot or neutral depending on the way in which they alter the balance of

*qi* within the body. The taste and smell of a herb are also important. Some are identified as pungent, others as sweet, yet others as bitter, salty or astringent. In the five element theory, these characteristics are related to various organs or body systems and to emotions.

Once the remedy has been prepared the practitioner will give you precise instructions about how to take it. Most remedies are made up into teas from herbs or powders and drunk, but some are taken in their raw form and others can be processed in pills or ointments.

## Herbal medicine and your back

Chinese herbal medicine is normally used to treat back pain in conjunction with one or more of the forms of Traditional Chinese Medicine specifically recommended for back pain; these include acupressure, acupuncture, moxibustion or cupping.

Certain herbs are believed to have antispasmodic, anti-inflammatory or painkilling effects but the complex and individually tailored nature of diagnosis and treatment in Traditional Chinese Medicine makes the comprehensive listing of back pain remedies difficult, as there are simply too many variables. The chart gives examples of herbs that might feature, among many others, in a traditional Chinese herbal remedy for back pain. A typical remedy can include up to 20 different herbs.

## CUPPING

*Rounded cups are used in this therapy, which is used to treat various conditions, including back, neck and shoulder pain.*

*A flame is held briefly inside the cup to burn up all the oxygen in the air. The flame is removed and the cup is quickly placed on the skin, creating a vacuum inside the cup, which causes the cup to stick tightly to the skin. The cup is left in place for up to half an hour during which time its internal vacuum draws up the skin into the cup, increasing blood circulation.*

## CHINESE HERBS FOR BACK PAIN

| REMEDY | |
|---|---|
| WU JIA PI (*Acanthopanax*) | "Wind-cold-damp" arthritis, especially in the elderly |
| SHU DI HUANG (prepared *Rehmennia* root) | Weak, sore lower back |
| HE SHOU WU (*Fleeceflower* root) | Weak lower back |
| DANG GUI (Chinese *Angelica* root) | Arthritis, traumatic injury – reduces swelling |
| CHUAN XIONG (Szechuan *Lovage* root) | Stiffness due to arthritis |
| DU ZHONG (*Eucommia* bark) | Lower back pain in pregnancy, general lower back pain – strengthens tendons and bones |
| GUI ZHI (cinnamon twigs) | Rheumatic complaints, especially in the shoulders |

A herbal remedy will take into account not only your symptoms but also your personality, physical constitution and even your likes and dislikes. Consult your doctor before acting on any of the suggestions in this book.

# Herbal medicine

*T*he earliest peoples would have learned the benefits – and dangers – of various plants through trial and error and from observing animals eating particular types of vegetation when unwell. This knowledge of herbal medicine was passed down through successive generations and is still used today.

*The medicinal effects of plants were carefully documented and classified in medieval Europe. This illustration of a liquorice plant is from* The Medieval Health Handbook *of 1380.*

Modern pharmaceutical-based medicine began in 1834, with the invention of the gelatin capsule. The new pharmacists took many traditional medicinal plants, extracted the therapeutic ingredient, processed it, encased it in a gelatin capsule and the modern drug was created. For example, the heart drug digitalis originally came from foxgloves.

The advent of modern drugs virtually killed off traditional herbal medicine. It is only in recent years, as people have become more concerned with the side effects of modern drugs, that there has been a resurgence of interest in herbalism.

Herbal medicine is a holistic therapy in which a person's lifestyle, environment, personality and emotions are taken into account along with his or her symptoms. Through the ages, different traditions of herbal medicine have developed systems of diagnosis and treatment.

In general, herbal practitioners believe plants have specific properties. Some are cooling, others are warming, some are relaxing, others stimulating and so forth. Different plants are believed to have affinities with different organs and bodily systems and can be used to promote the body's natural ability to heal itself.

In the West today, herbalists are more likely to choose plants for their medicinal effects as opposed to other more general properties. However, although schools of herbal medicine may differ in methods of diagnosis and treatment, they all still share one

important, fundamental belief – that the strength of the sum of the parts is greater than the strength of any of the individual parts of a plant. For this reason, herbalists, unlike pharmacists, use the whole of a plant in their remedies.

Pharmaceuticals are manufactured by identifying the ingredient in a plant that acts against a particular condition or disease, extracting it and processing it into pills or tablets. This results in drugs that act far more powerfully against disease than the original plant could. Many drugs are so powerful that they are poisonous to the human body. This toxicity may lead to unpleasant side effects. For many drugs the line between being therapeutic and poisonous is very narrow and some, especially those used to treat cancers, may only be effective at doses that are also poisonous to the rest of the body.

Herbalists argue that the active ingredient is just one of hundreds of constituents of each plant and that these other constituents dampen the effect of the active one, allowing the plant to be therapeutic without being toxic. A prime example they point to is aspirin, which was originally processed from the bark of the willow tree. It is an effective painkiller and anti-inflammatory drug but its use is often limited because it irritates the lining of the stomach. Willow bark, however, rarely causes such problems – herbalists sometimes use it to treat stomach problems.

As a result, there is a popular view that pharmaceuticals are powerful and have nasty side effects whereas herbal remedies are gentle and have no side effects. This is a fine idea, but it is not altogether true. Herbal remedies share the same active ingredients as many drugs and in fact they can be dangerous if used incorrectly – you should always seek the advice of a qualified herbalist.

## Herbal medicine in practice

Herbal remedies are prepared in various ways. One of the most common is infusion, known as *tisane* in France. Here the plant or plants are steeped in hot water for about 15 minutes, in much the same way as brewing a pot of tea. The liquid is strained off and drunk hot or cold. Alternatively, tinctures are made by chopping up the plant and soaking it in a solution of three-quarters water and one-quarter alcohol and leaving it to stand for up to two weeks. The liquid is drained off and taken as medicine by mouth. Herbal remedies can also be used in compresses, poultices, gargles, inhalations, and in creams and ointments.

Various herbal remedies are believed to help ease problems such as muscular tension and joint inflammation which can cause back pain. The chart here is included as a general guide only – advice should always be sought from a qualified therapist before embarking upon a course of herbal medication.

## HERBAL REMEDIES FOR BACK PROBLEMS

| REMEDY | MAIN USE |
|---|---|
| CAYENNE | Inflammation and pain (external use only) |
| CHAMOMILE | Inflammation (external use only) |
| CHINESE FOXGLOVE ROOT | Low back pain |
| CIMICIFUGA | Inflammation |
| MEADOWSWEET | Rheumatic pain |
| SIBERIAN GINSENG | Inflammation |
| NOTOGINSENG ROOT | Swelling and pain (external use only) |
| TURMERIC | Arthritis pain (external use only) |
| VERVAIN | General pain |
| YARROW | Inflammation |

NOTE The information and recommendations given in this book are not intended to be a substitute for medical advice. Consult your doctor before acting on any of the suggestions in this book.

# Alexander technique

*F*inding a therapy that eases or cures your back trouble is wonderful, but discovering a way of preventing it ever recurring is even better. The Alexander technique, which focuses on good posture, provides just such a way.

It is evident that posture plays an important role in many cases of simple back pain. Years of standing, walking and sitting badly, so that the spine and the rest of the body are out of balance, may lead to joint and muscle strain and eventually chronic back pain. The Alexander technique aims to improve posture – and in so doing may eliminate some of the causes of back pain.

The technique's founder, Tasmanian-born actor Frederick Matthias Alexander, began to develop the technique in an attempt to cure the temporary loss of his voice. Alexander, who was born in 1869, noticed that his voice loss only occurred after a period on stage and set up an elaborate system of mirrors to watch what he did when he spoke on stage. He noticed that he involuntarily contracted the muscles in his head and neck, which affected his breathing. He wondered whether keeping these muscles relaxed would help him recover his voice and he set about trying to achieve this.

By altering his posture and paying particular attention to the relationship between his head, neck and spine, Alexander recovered and improved his voice and breath control. Alexander had discovered what he called the primary control mechanism. When the head, neck and spine are properly aligned, the rest of the body is brought into a state of balance or harmony and is able to carry out everyday activities with a minimum of strain.

During the 1930s Alexander's ideas gained an international following, first among fellow actors who sought his advice, but later among many prominent doctors and other well-known figures. Today there are training centres for Alexander technique teachers throughout Europe and the United States.

Alexander lessons teach the coordination of posture, breathing and voice control and are extremely popular with public speakers, dancers, singers, musicians and actors. Many colleges of music and drama have classes in Alexander technique and it is also frequently used by clinics that specialize in pain control. Some scientific research into Alexander technique supports both

*Lying down with some head support – books may help your neck stay in alignment better than a pillow – and your knees raised allows your spine to rest flat against the floor. This is a useful way of releasing tension from your body.*

its theoretical basis and its practical benefits for a wide range of physical problems, including back and neck pain.

## The technique in practice

The simple, fundamental theory behind Alexander technique is that the way in which you use your body affects how well it functions. Alexander also knew how hard it was to break bad habits. He believed that constantly trying to take action to correct poor posture could do more harm than good and would probably lead to further injury. Instead, he realized that poor posture could only be overcome by relearning how to stand, walk, sit and move.

Lessons or classes in Alexander technique usually last for about an hour at a time. The aim is to re-educate you and make you think consciously about the way you move and hold your body. Eventually, beneficial posture becomes part of a natural life, whether you are walking, sitting, writing a letter, working or simply lying on the floor reading a book. The basics are usually taught over a series of about 10 classes, and lessons are offered on a one-to-one basis.

At first the teacher will observe how you perform simple actions, such as walking across the room, then use his or her hands to guide you gently into correct postures. If poor posture habits have become ingrained over the years you may find that the correct way to stand or sit initially feels wrong and unnatural. You may find that your teacher spends the whole of one lesson watching you repeat a simple action, such as sitting down in a chair and standing up again or walking across the room. Gradually, you completely relearn the way in which you move and think about movement.

## Helping your back

The Alexander technique can be of great benefit to individuals suffering both from generalized chronic back and neck pain and from specific problems such as sciatica and brachialgia. The emphasis on the correct coordination between good posture and relaxed breathing helps prevent the build-up of mental and physical tension that is so often the cause of back pain.

The technique is used for a wide range of problems but especially for stress-related conditions, including high blood pressure, anxiety, depression and insomnia, and for breathing disorders such as asthma.

The technique is safe for use by children but few need it. Those who have spinal problems, however, are often helped by classes. It is also safe during pregnancy, when changing body shape and the pressure on the spine often cause back problems.

*It is important to receive instruction from an Alexander teacher, who will show you the correct ways to stand and sit.*

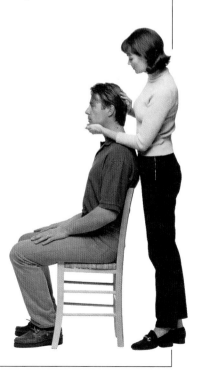

# Reflexology

*A* *nyone who has experienced a foot massage at the end of a long day knows how pleasant and relaxing it can be. Reflexology, or reflex zone therapy, is a specialized foot massage based on a system of energy pathways.*

It is likely that reflexology as it is practised today has its roots in ancient China, along with acupressure and acupuncture. There is also archaeological evidence from ancient Egypt and ancient Greece which indicates that foot massage may have been used as a therapy by physicians at the time. Foot massage for healing was also common among the native peoples of North and South America.

Reflexologists view the underside of the foot as a chart of the human body. They believe that it is divided up into different areas, or reflex zones, that are directly connected to specific organs and structures, such as the spine, shoulders and head. They maintain that illness and disease are the result of energy imbalances in specific organs or body structures and that these imbalances are reflected in the corresponding area on the soles of the feet. By massaging these areas, a reflexologist can detect and then correct the problem, clearing the way for the body to heal itself.

Modern reflexology was developed during the early part of the 20th century by two Americans – the physician Dr William Fitzgerald and Eunice Ingham, who continued his work. Fitzgerald first proposed the idea that the body was divided into 10 zones, starting at the head and ending at the toes, and that these zones were reflected on the soles of the feet. Ingham elaborated on this basic theory and developed the now familiar reflexology chart showing the zones on the soles of the feet and areas of the body to which they correspond.

## Reflexology in practice

A reflexology session typically lasts up to an hour. The practitioner will ask you about your symptoms and then spend some time examining your feet. Treatment often begins with the practitioner dusting your feet with talcum powder and giving them a gentle, all-over massage. Problem areas can often be identified at this stage because they feel tender or sore. The practitioner will then use his or her thumbs to massage these areas. It may be slightly painful at first but this sensation soon disappears as treatment progresses and is often replaced by a feeling of relaxation and wellbeing.

Most reflexologists maintain that several sessions are needed before the full effects of reflexology are felt. As the

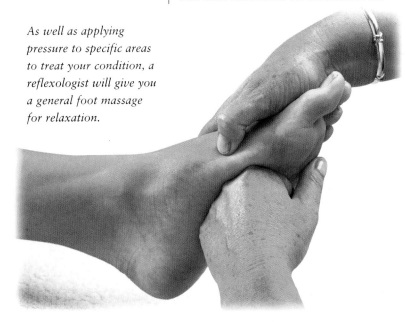

*As well as applying pressure to specific areas to treat your condition, a reflexologist will give you a general foot massage for relaxation.*

treatment takes effect you may experience what reflexologists describe as cleansing reactions such as a headache, sweating, diarrhoea and an increased desire to urinate. Practitioners attribute this to an increase in the efficiency of the body's elimination system as a result of the treatment and view it as a good sign.

## Feet and back

There is no agreed scientific theory as to how reflexology works, but many people report that it helps back problems, including neck pain and sciatica. A reflexologist might treat neck pain by pressing on the base of the big toe, the zone that corresponds to the neck. In the same way, back pain could be treated by applying pressure to the inside edges of the big toes and all along the inside of the foot as this is thought to correspond to the spine.

The zone corresponding to the bladder may also be massaged as this is believed to be linked to the supporting

muscles and ligaments that run up and down the length of the spine. Stimulation of this zone will therefore relieve the problem of associated pain. Zones corresponding to the sciatic nerve are located toward the bottom of the foot, close to the heel.

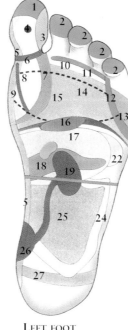

RIGHT FOOT    LEFT FOOT

**REFLEXOLOGY POINTS**

*Each area of the foot corresponds to a specific organ or part of the body. The right foot relates to the right side and the left foot to the left side of the body.*

1 Brain/top of head
2 Sinuses
3 Side of neck
4 Pituitary gland
5 Spine
6 Neck/throat/thyroid
7 Parathyroid
8 Thyroid
9 Trachea
10 Eye
11 Eustachian tube
12 Ear
13 Shoulder
14 Lung
15 Heart
16 Solar plexus
17 Stomach
18 Pancreas
19 Kidney
20 Liver
21 Gall bladder
22 Spleen
23 Ascending colon
24 Descending colon
25 Small intestine
26 Bladder
27 Sciatic nerve

## VACUFLEX

*A high-tech version of reflexology that uses a vacuum pump and suction is vacuflex, or the vacuflex reflexology system. It was developed by Danish reflexologist Inge Douglas and has been used to the benefit of many people who have not responded to standard reflexology.*

*In this therapy you wear a pair of special vacuum boots. The air is pumped out and the boots squeeze your feet, stimulating all the reflex zones at*

*once. The boots are then removed and any areas of discoloration on your feet are said to reveal areas of imbalance. The discolorations fade after 20 or 30 seconds but this gives the practitioner time to assess the state of your health.*

*Once problem areas have been identified, the practitioner uses small suction pads to stimulate the specific reflex points that need attention. This stimulation is said to unblock the energy pathways.*

# Psychotherapy and counselling

*A*ll complementary therapies view the human body from a holistic perspective. Practitioners believe that the whole person – mind, body and spirit – needs to be considered in order to understand and treat ill-health.

*Psychotherapy has its roots in the pioneering work of Sigmund Freud in the late 19th and early 20th century. Followers of Freud practise a form of therapy known as pyschoanalysis.*

Practitioners of complementary medicine have long recognized the intimate relationship between mind and body and understood that psychological factors influence physical health and vice versa. On a simple level, everyday experience demonstrates this relationship. When you feel sad or depressed minor health problems seem to be magnified, and during periods of illness, when you are suffering a heavy cold, for example, you tend to feel depressed.

Doctors working in conventional medicine now recognize the importance of such a holistic approach. They accept that psychological factors, including worry, suppressed anger and frustration, long-term stress and anxiety, play a large role in many physical conditions, including back and neck pain, asthma, eczema, migraine and irritable bowel syndrome. They recognize that long-term illness can lead to psychological problems, especially depression and related disorders.

## Counselling

Most people have experienced the relief of talking over their problems with a trusted friend. There is a lot of truth in the old saying "A problem shared is a problem halved." Talking about a problem is a vital part of recognizing it, solving it – or, if that is not possible, accepting it – and moving on.

For most of human history this has been the accepted way of dealing with worries, anxieties and stress. In large, extended families comprising individuals of several generations grouped into closely knit communities, there was always someone able to give support and a sympathetic ear.

However, in today's busy, individualistic and largely urban Western society many people live relatively isolated lives. A consequence of this is that finding someone outside your immediate family in whom to confide is not easy. Often it is better to have a professional listener,

---

### BIOENERGETICS

*The work of Austrian psychotherapist Wilhelm Reich, in the first part of the 20th century, gave rise to bioenergetics. He believed that people unconsciously tense their muscles to protect themselves against mental pain and anguish, and this tension becomes locked into the body, affecting posture and patterns of breathing.*

*This means that an individual's posture and movements reflects his or her underlying psychological and emotional state. Therapists are trained to read the messages of the body and use a combination of psychological and physical techniques to bring out and resolve the underlying mental pain, allowing the body to function again in a proper, balanced way.*

someone who is not emotionally close to you and who is able to give a more detached and objective opinion of your problems. This is what a counsellor does.

Today, counselling is an established and widespread therapy with a recognized role in the treatment of many chronic conditions and illnesses. Some counsellors practise privately from home while others are employed by clinics and hospitals. Counsellors provide a sympathetic and practical listening ear in a safe environment that will allow you as a client to talk about and sort out any problems you may have.

## Psychotherapy

This is a form of treatment that explores unconscious issues and feelings and their effect on thought and behaviour. It is not the same as psychiatry, a branch of conventional medicine; psychiatrists are medically trained doctors who use drugs as part of their treatments.

Psychotherapists are not doctors and do not prescribe drugs. They "treat" their clients by listening and talking to them – and in some cases working with them using methods such as role play – to identify underlying problems and help solve them.

**Find out more**

| | |
|---|---|
| *Psychological stress* | *52* |
| *Choosing a therapy* | *82* |
| *Finding a practitioner* | *146* |

## THE MAIN SCHOOLS OF PSYCHOTHERAPY

| | |
|---|---|
| ANALYTICAL | This is the form of psychotherapy developed by Freud and Jung, which maintains that many problems are the result of unresolved and suppressed childhood experiences. The analyst tries to uncover these early experiences and find a way of helping you deal with them. |
| HUMANISTIC | Humanistic psychotherapy developed from the optimism that followed the end of World War II and the rejection of many of the established and authoritarian social norms that had constrained individuals until that time. Therapists subscribing to this method favour self-knowledge and self-determination, and maintain that we all have choices. As long as we are willing to take responsibility for ourselves and our actions, we can change our lives for the better. |
| BEHAVIOURAL | Behavioural therapy was introduced at the beginning of the 20th century. Its fundamental concept is that people can learn to react to life's problems in a positive, rather than a negative, way. It concentrates on practical ways of achieving this and encourages individuals to confront difficult situations and learn new reactions to them. |
| INTEGRATIVE | Therapies belonging to the integrative school aim to integrate mind, body and soul and use a mixture of humanistic approaches and elements from some of the other schools of psychotherapy. Transactional analysis, based on the "games people play", is perhaps the best known integrative therapy. Developed in the United States by Eric Berne during the 1950s, transactional analysis is based on the theory that every social situation is a transaction in which individuals present a selected facet of their personality in order to achieve certain ends. Therapists analyse these transactions in terms of whether the individual is playing the role of child, parent or adult and what goals they are trying to achieve by adopting such roles. |

# Other bodywork techniques

*D*uring *the 20th century, several individuals, influenced by osteopathy and chiropractic, have developed bodywork techniques that draw on and elaborate the basic principles of those therapies.*

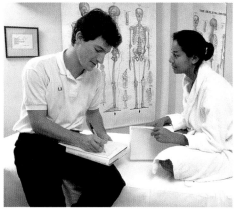

*As well as manipulating specific areas of the body, a Rolfing practitioner provides instruction in using the body efficiently.*

## Rolfing

Many complementary therapies that are effective in treating back pain stress the importance of the correct alignment of the body's supporting structures – the bones, ligaments, muscles and tendons.

This is also the theory behind Rolfing. Named after its founder, American biologist Dr Ida Rolf, Rolfing combines elements of osteopathy, Alexander technique and shiatsu. The technique grew out of Dr Rolf's fascination with both manipulative therapy and the flow of energy within the body.

She observed that when the body's structures were properly aligned, it functioned gracefully and efficiently and without excessive effort. If, however, any part of the structure became misaligned, other areas came under excessive strain as they tried to compensate and, eventually, the whole system was thrown out of balance, leading to strain, injury and pain.

*A Hellerwork session includes a massage to realign the musculoskeletal system and ease muscular tension.*

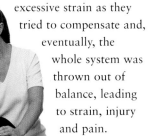

Rolfing aims to realign the whole body using a variety of massage techniques. Practitioners believe that once the supporting structures are realigned, the mind and nervous system operate more efficiently and the body's natural healing energy is able to begin its work. Like osteopaths and chiropractors, Rolfing practitioners often deal with structural problems. The therapy is sometimes used to treat other conditions, such as asthma, migraine, fatigue, digestion and menstrual problems.

A full course of therapy consists of 10 or more sessions, each lasting an hour or so. During each session the practitioner concentrates on a specific area of the body so that eventually the whole body is believed to be correctly aligned.

## Hellerwork

Invented by Joseph Heller in the United States during the 1970s, Hellerwork is a development of Rolfing. The technique uses manipulation and massage, as well as movement re-education with the help of video feedback. Like Rolfing, Hellerwork aims to realign the supporting structures of the body and promote self-healing. Practitioners also spend a considerable amount of time talking with the person they are treating in order to reinforce the link between mind and body.

## Feldenkrais method

In common with other complementary therapies, the Feldenkrais method is adapted to you, and not the other way around. Practitioners of this technique concentrate on developing and enhancing the posture that they believe is naturally correct for you.

Like Frederick Matthias Alexander, founder of the Alexander technique, Moshe Feldenkrais held that posture and correct movement could be the key to good health. An Israeli engineer and physicist, Feldenkrais began to investigate body mechanics in order to relieve the pain of a long-standing knee injury. The result was the Feldenkrais method, a form of physical therapy that combines elements of yoga, stretching, and the Alexander technique.

The fundamental theory behind Feldenkrais' work was that the body could "reprogramme" the mind. Feldenkrais, who died in 1984 at the age of 80, believed that physically manipulating the body to encourage it to move in better, more efficient ways fed the information directly into the nervous system, enabling the individual to learn new patterns of movement relatively rapidly.

Today, the Feldenkrais method is used to treat people with serious movement and physical disabilities. Its benefits are also being felt by a growing number of sportsmen and women, as well as performers such as dancers and musicians.

The Feldenkrais method is taught in two forms. In the first form, known as functional integration, a teacher works on a one-to-one basis with a client. Sessions last for about an hour, during which time the teacher uses specialized manipulation techniques to show the client how to move his or her body with maximum efficiency and minimum effort.

The second form, known as awareness through movement, is taught in groups. Under the practitioner's guidance, students are asked to perform and concentrate on a series of movements.

In this way, they become aware of the patterns of muscular tension that are thought to be caused by moving in an inefficient manner and learn how to avoid this by moving correctly.

The Feldenkrais method has been shown to help a wide range of health problems, especially musculoskeletal conditions such as back pain, spinal problems, arthritis and chronic pain.

## Warning

As with other manipulative therapies, you should not undergo Rolfing, Hellerwork or Feldenkrais if you suffer from any disease or condition that directly affects the strength of the bones or joints, such as osteoporosis, rheumatoid arthritis and cancer of the bones. You should always discuss your health fully with the practitioner before agreeing to any treatment.

*A Feldenkrais practitioner applies gentle massage to encourage body awareness.*

*Manipulation during a Feldenkrais session is intended to improve a joint's range of motion.*

# Environmental medicine

*There is growing evidence that environmental factors, especially food allergies and intolerances, can cause aching and painful muscles in the back and elsewhere in the body. Clinical ecology or environmental medicine includes a variety of techniques to test for allergies and to analyse environmental influences on individual health.*

*Dairy products are among the most common causes of food allergies, affecting about one person in five.*

*An intolerance to gluten, a protein found in wheat and wheat products, has been implicated in many health problems, including chronic fatigue and pain.*

The idea that an individual's everyday environment can affect his or her health is a fundamental concept in modern complementary medicine. Clinical ecologists believe that a large number of people are allergic to everyday foods such as milk and wheat products.

However, the modern world also contains many other challenges to people's health. Most of our food is sprayed with pesticides, more and more people are eating so-called junk food and meals full of preservatives, and air quality is decreasing as traffic volumes increase.

Some experts in environmental medicine now estimate that anything up to one-third of the population of the world's developed nations suffer from some form of environmentally induced ill-health, including headaches, aches and pains, asthma and skin problems such as eczema.

If you live in a big town there may be little you can do to avoid some of these hazards, but it is worth cutting down on foods that contain high amounts of chemical preservatives, just in case your back pain is part of an allergic reaction.

## Allergy testing

The simplest way to test for food allergies is the elimination or exclusion diet. This involves cutting out substances from your diet for one or two weeks and then reintroducing them one at a time to see if they cause an adverse reaction. Seek advice from a qualified nutritionist or dietician to make sure you are still eating balanced meals and getting all the nutrients you need.

Applied kinesiology is an allergy-testing technique based on the theory that substances to which a person is sensitive cause muscle weakening by interfering with the body's electrical field. Suspect substances are placed under the person's tongue or in the hand and practitioners check for tell-tale weakness.

Another test that involves the body's electrical field is known as auricular cardiac reflex. Practitioners check for changes in a person's pulse when foods suspected of causing an allergic reaction are placed within the electrical field.

In intradermal testing, suspect substances are diluted and a little of the liquid is injected under the skin to see if it causes an allergic reaction.

# Ayurvedic medicine

*Originated in India some 5,000 years ago, ayurveda is a holistic system of health promotion, disease prevention and treatment. Practitioners of Ayurvedic medicine view the body as microcosm of the universe.*

The name Ayurveda comes from the Sanskrit words *ayur*, which means life or lifespan, and *veda*, which means knowledge or wholeness of knowledge. Like Traditional Chinese Medicine, Ayurvedic medicine is based on the concept of a life-force. In Ayurveda it is known as *prana*.

Practitioners believe that good health depends on the correct flow of *prana* through the body. This, in turn, relies on a proper balance between three basic forces, known as *doshas*, which control all physical and mental functions. These forces are *pitta*, *vata* and *kapha*.

*Pitta*, linked to the sun, is the source of energy that controls digestion and all the body's biochemical processes. *Vata*, linked to the wind, controls the nervous system and movement. *Kapha*, linked to the moon, governs cell and tissue growth and bodily structures.

In Ayurvedic medicine, the universe consists of five elements: space or ether, air, fire, water and earth. The elements are related to the five senses – hearing, touch, sight, taste and smell, respectively. They also relate to the body's organs and systems, with a disturbance in an element prompting a disorder in the corresponding body system.

Ayurveda practitioners take a detailed history of an person's health before making a physical examination. Attention is also paid to lifestyle factors, such as diet, and the person's emotional state.

Diet and digestion are of fundamental importance in Ayurvedic medicine and

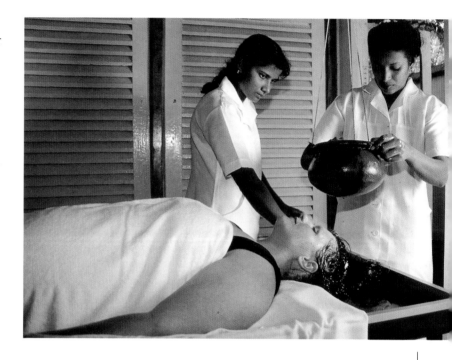

practitioners view problems in these areas as a major cause of disease. Foods are seen as providing intelligence, order and balance as well as physical nourishment, and different foods have different effects on the *doshas*. Food is used to rebalance the *doshas*. Diets are designed for each individual. These take into account the type of *dosha* imbalance, the person's symptoms, the weather and the of year.

Controlling the diet in this manner – combined with fasting – and advice on breathing techniques, relaxation and meditation are often enough to relieve any symptoms. However, if the condition persists practitioners may introduce herbal remedies, massage, enemas, crystals and colour therapy.

*As an initial aid to detoxification, an Ayurvedic practitioner may suggest a steam bath, or a massage using herbal oils. Herbal inhalation therapy may also be suggested.*

# Healing

*The kirlian photographic image results from the interaction between the subject and an applied electrical field. Light emitted as photons from the electrical interaction causes the image on film.*

*Every culture in the world has legendary healers, many of whom were also religious leaders and teachers. Today this tradition continues to flourish and spiritual or psychic healing is one of the most popular complementary therapies.*

Psychic healing is based on the concept of a universal healing energy. Different cultures see this energy in different ways. The concept of a universal, life-giving energy has been part of Eastern medicine and philosophy for thousands of years.

In Western psychic healing traditions, this healing energy is known as the subtle body. It is said to consist of several energy fields that radiate from the body, surrounding it. The energy fields are believed to be related to a person's physical, mental and spiritual dimensions. Many Western healers believe that the subtle body is the essence of the Christian Holy Spirit.

Psychic healers work in different ways. Some touch the person being healed while others work in the energy field. Some use colour and sound, others crystals, and yet others combine psychic healing with various types of massage. Psychic healers maintain that they are able to help any condition and chronic problems such as back pain can respond well. However, they point out that results depend heavily on the relationship between healer and client.

Many psychic healers are also trained counsellors. They stress that most people can benefit from psychic healing but warn that progress is often gradual.

# Reiki

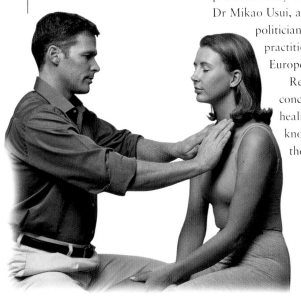

Reiki (pronounced "ray-kee") as it is practised today was largely developed by Dr Mikao Usui, a 19th-century Japanese politician. Today, there are Reiki practitioners throughout Europe and North America. Reiki is based on the concept of a universal healing energy. Teachers, known as masters, pass their knowledge on to pupils through a series of three "degrees". The first enables the pupil to transmit healing energy to him or herself and to others, the second reinforces this ability and enables the pupil to undertake healing over long distances. The third degree entitles those receiving it to teach others.

Some Reiki practitioners touch the person being healed; others work in the energy fields surrounding the body. Once the first degree has been achieved, Reiki can be used as a self-help technique and daily treatment is recommended as way of promoting health and spiritual growth

The effectiveness of Reiki depends on the relationship between healer and the person being healed. It is important that the subject participates fully in the session and is in a receptive frame of mind. Practitioners say that Reiki helps all conditions and illnesses and is particularly suited to treating chronic problems such as back pain.

# Crystal therapy

At the more controversial end of the complementary healing spectrum, crystal therapy is criticized for its lack of a scientific basis. Its proponents, however, believe in the healing power of crystals and have achieved positive results.

While there is no scientific basis for any of the healing claims made by crystal therapy, some people with chronic conditions – such as back pain – report that they do seem to be helped by the presence of various crystals. If the idea of using crystals appeals to you, it is worth trying the therapy for yourself to see if it works for you.

According to practitioners, gems and crystals emit vibrations that are beneficial to health. Placed on an individual's body or within their subtle body – the fields of energy believed by some to surround every person – they can absorb negative, harmful energy and enhance positive, healing energy. Gems and crystals can also be immersed in water, which is said to absorb their energies. When the water is drunk it promotes self-healing.

Uncut stones are believed to have a more powerful effect than cut and polished gems and crystals. Gems and crystals should be cleaned with sea salt and washed with fresh water before being used for healing. They should then be washed regularly in clean water and recharged by being left in direct sunlight for several hours.

## Electrocrystal therapy

Developed by UK practitioner Harry Oldfield in the 1970s, electrocrystal therapy is said to work by rebalancing the flow of universal healing energy through the body. Therapists subscribe to the philosophy of meridians (as in Traditional Chinese Medicine) through which this energy flows. Crystals are sealed inside brine-filled glass tubes, which are placed on specific meridians. A weak electrical current is then passed through the tubes. Practitioners believe that this sets up a healing vibration that is passed into the body of the subject.

## SOME STONES AND CRYSTALS

| CRYSTAL | DESCRIPTION | BENEFITS |
|---|---|---|
| FLUORITE | Violet crystals (also in other colours) | Helps physical and mental coordination |
| JASPER | Opaque quartz in many colours | Gently activates all the body's functions |
| MALACHITE | Green crystals of copper carbonate | Restores harmony and balance |
| ROSE QUARTZ | Pink, translucent, usually small crystals | Balances the heart and emotions |
| CITRINE | Golden-yellow or orange-brown stone | Keeps the mind focused; energizing |

Fluorite    Jasper    Malachite    Rose quartz    Citrine

# Finding a practitioner

*O*nce you have decided on a therapy to try to relieve your back pain, the next step is to find a reliable practitioner. Probably the best way to do this is to ask around and get personal recommendation from friends or your doctor.

*For a treatment to be effective, you need to feel at ease and have complete trust in your therapist.*

If you are looking for an osteopath or chiropractor, try asking your family doctor. You could also try this route for counselling and psychotherapy – and possibly even Alexander technique. If you want to find a reflexologist or a crystal therapist, however, you would probably be well advised to ask elsewhere.

A personal recommendation is often the best way of finding a reliable practitioner. Local health-food shops are often a goldmine of information about complementary practitioners in the area, as are pharmacies. Many have noticeboards advertising various therapies but ask the staff as well, since many of the better known practitioners do not need to advertise.

It is also worth looking at noticeboards in supermarkets, libraries and leisure or sports centres.

You can also try the local telephone directory under the therapy of your choice. Many practitioners now advertise their services in this way and you may find there is a natural health centre offering therapies in your area.

Another approach is to contact a self-help group. These groups, run by and for those suffering from a particular condition, vary hugely in size and sophistication, from local groups with a handful of members to national organizations with expertly staffed advice lines. Many publish regular newsletters with the latest information about therapies and keep lists of recommended practitioners. They are often listed in the telephone directory but, if not, your local library is an excellent place to start looking for a suitable therapist.

On a national scale, you can often obtain a list of practitioners in any particular therapy from its umbrella organization. As complementary

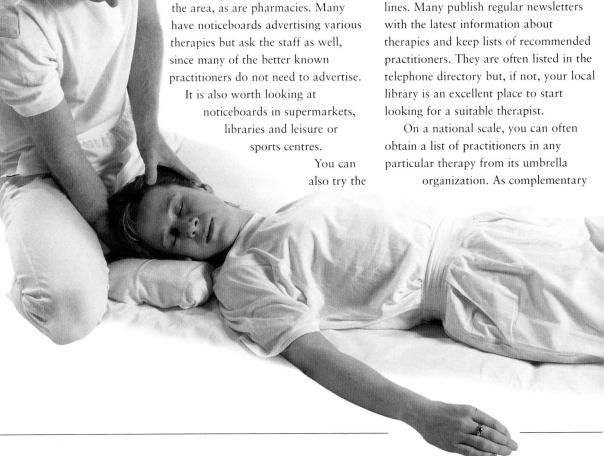

medicine becomes more established, there is an increasing number of professional and umbrella organizations that represent practitioners of different therapies.

Some of these are professional bodies in the true sense in that they lay down the qualifications needed by members and take an active role in training and ongoing education. Others are simply associations which any practitioner in that field is entitled to join and are really little more than a list of members' names and addresses. It is worth checking when you contact a particular organization which of these two categories it falls into. If it is the former, then you can be fairly confident that its members will all be properly qualified.

Once you have found a suitable practitioner your first visit will give you a pretty good idea about whether he or she is reliable and whether you wish to carry on with the therapy. Trust your instincts here. The practitioner should give you a feeling of confidence. It is important to remember that the success of many complementary therapies depends, to a large extent, on a nurturing relationship between healer and the person being healed. You are in charge and if you do not feel at ease with the practitioner or think that you may not get along with him or her, do not worry about saying so and leaving.

For manipulative therapies, the practitioner's touch should be firm and professional, yet sensitive and gentle at all times. No practitioner should ever touch you in an intimate area without first asking permission and explaining exactly why it is necessary. If you are uneasy about this, ask to have a friend present during the session. No bona fide practitioner will object – if they do, find another therapist.

No genuine practitioner will ask for payment in advance unless in exceptional circumstances, perhaps for special tests or medicines. If this is the case ask the practitioner to explain exactly what the money is for and if you are not happy with the explanation, refuse to pay and find another therapist.

**Find out more**

*Choosing a therapy*　　　84
*Helpful organizations*　　170

## PRACTITIONER CHECKLIST

• *Ensure that your therapist has taken an accredited course of training.*

• *Ask to be put in touch with satisfied clients.*

• *Check with your doctor before starting any unorthodox therapy.*

• *Check your therapist's qualifications, training and experience with their governing body, if there is one.*

• *Check whether your therapist is happy to work with your doctor, and whether treatment is covered under health insurance schemes.*

• *Insist on knowing in advance how many sessions of treatment you are likely to need, and how much this is likely to cost.*

• *Ask precisely how the treatment offered is likely to benefit you.*

• *Always beware of any hard-sell methods or attempts to make you buy expensive extras, such as supplements, books and videos.*

• *Never book sessions with any practitioner who claims to be able to cure your condition for ever.*

# Conventional therapies

*As a back-pain sufferer, you have a wide choice of therapies. Many people can testify to the effectiveness of complementary medicine. But for some, conventional treatment may be preferable.*

Most people do not deliberately choose conventional medicine. When they are ill they go to see their family doctor. In many countries consulting your family doctor is free of charge and it is the route to reassurance that they are not seriously ill.

Despite the growing popularity of complementary therapies, for most people they are still just that – complementary to conventional medicine. Most people suffering their first bout of serious back pain visit their doctor to be examined, reassured and, if necessary, treated. It is only if the problem persists and conventional treatment fails that many people start thinking about consulting an osteopath/chiropractor or some other therapist. In the case of osteopathy or chiropractic, the doctor may suggest this and be able to recommend an individual to a suitable practitioner.

If you are suffering from severe back pain for the first time and your symptoms do not clear up within a week or so it is a good idea to consult your doctor, even if it is only to rule out any serious underlying condition. You can then decide what sort of treatment you would like. If you are suffering from a recurrence of back pain and have consulted your doctor in the past, it is still worth finding out whether conventional treatment may be appropriate now.

# Investigations for back pain

*In the vast majority of cases, a combination of activity and medication to ease the pain and unlock muscular spasm will be all you need to heal your back pain. But if the pain does not go away, or if it keeps recurring, your doctor may refer you to a specialist for further investigation.*

*An X-ray can show damage to bones, but not to cartilage, ligaments or muscles. A metal splint on a fractured spine is seen clearly in thisX-ray.*

### Consulting your family doctor

When you first consult your family doctor about your back pain, he or she will probably spend a few minutes asking you about your specific symptoms as well your general state of health.

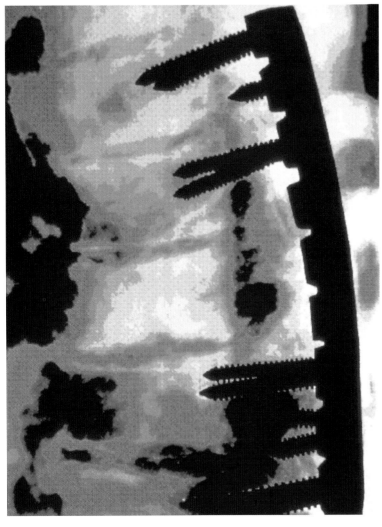

The doctor will then examine you and reach a preliminary diagnosis. If the doctor rules out the likelihood of any serious illness or structural problem he or she will probably advise you to keep active and may prescribe one or more of the following types of drugs: painkillers, anti-inflammatory drugs and/or muscle relaxants and, possibly, antidepressants.

If this treatment does not succeed in giving your back the opportunity to heal itself, it will be necessary to undergo further investigation.

### Consulting a specialist

The specialist's role is to find out whether your pain is a symptom of a physical disease or condition in your back or elsewhere in the body and, if not, to discover exactly what is causing it. The specialist, usually an orthopaedic surgeon, a rheumatologist or a neurologist, will spend some time taking a careful history of your symptoms and your general health. He or she will then give you a thorough physical examination, looking at your posture and investigating how much movement your spine can make and how well it makes these movements. He or she will probably also manipulate your arms, legs and neck to check for signs of nerve root obstruction.

X-rays are rarely helpful in diagnosing the cause of back pain as the muscles, ligaments and discs do not show up at all or show only very faintly. As result, a condition such as a prolapsed disc could easily be missed by an X-ray. The only clue might be a slight narrowing of the space between two vertebrae but this can be hard to spot and does not necessarily indicate a prolapse. Because of this and because X-rays are known to carry some risks for health, far fewer are taken now than used to be the case.

The specialist will probably also take a blood sample which will be tested to rule out bone disease and other illnesses and conditions that can cause back pain. Depending on the results of the physical examination, X-rays and blood tests, the specialist will be able to make a diagnosis and recommend treatment.

If the specialist finds that the diagnosis is still unclear, further tests may be necessary (see box below). In the vast majority of cases, however, they are unnecessary and are normally only carried out if the specialist thinks that surgery might be needed. Always discuss with your specialist the reasons for any tests he recommends and make sure that you are happy it is necessary.

## SPECIALIST INVESTIGATIONS FOR BACK PAIN

**Myelography** *The aim of this test is to make the dural tube that surrounds and protects the spinal cord show up on X-ray. To achieve this, a contrast medium – a substance that shows up on an X-ray – is injected into the fluid surrounding the spinal cord under local anaesthetic. The X-rays will reveal whether anything is obstructing the spinal canal and putting pressure on the spinal cord or any of the nerve roots branching off from it.*

**Discography** *This is a similar procedure to myelography which aims to make discs visible on an X-ray. A contrast medium is injected into the centre of a suspected prolapsed disc. If the disc is healthy, the contrast medium stays in the centre but if it has ruptured, the X-ray will show the contrast medium spreading out and can therefore indicate the extent of the prolapse.*

**Magnetic resonance imaging (MRI)** *This procedure is a high-tech, non-invasive replacement for myelography. You lie inside a cylindrical machine that contains a powerful electromagnet. Using radio waves, the machine scans you and produces high-quality images of your body and internal organs and structures in cross-section.*

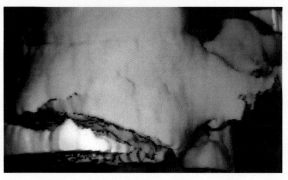

A profile of a spine pictured by a CT scan shows a wedge-shaped fracture to the body of a vertebra.

**Computerized tomography (CAT or CT scanning)** *A high-tech alternative to myelography. X-rays are taken from different angles and a computer analyses them and presents the information as cross-sections of the body.*

**Ultrasound** *This is a non-invasive procedure that can be used to build up a picture of the spine. A probe, which emits ultra-high frequency sound waves, is passed over the back. The waves bounce off the spine and are picked by again by the probe in much the same way as sonar is used to locate and identify underwater objects.*

# Physiotherapy

$M$*any people, used to a passive relationship with a health professional, are surprised to find that the physiotherapist expects them to work hard at getting better.*

*A physiotherapist will make sure that the treatment is appropriate to your particular condition.*

In most countries, state-registered, or licensed, physiotherapists are trained to degree level and work in hospitals, community clinics, industry, sports organizations and clubs and in private practice. Family doctors can refer people directly to a physiotherapist, but most are sent for this form of therapy by their hospital consultant.

As the demand for complementary medicine grows, some physiotherapists are broadening their skills and learning therapies such as acupuncture and aromatherapy. Regardless of whether or not a physiotherapist offers such therapies, there is a fundamental similarity between physiotherapy and complementary medicine – the patient takes an active role in the healing process.

### Seeing a physiotherapist

Physiotherapists are experts in their own field and although your doctor will have sent your medical notes, the results of any tests that have been performed and a diagnosis, he or she will leave the physiotherapist to decide what sort of treatment is the best for your condition.

At your first visit, the physiotherapist will spend a considerable amount of time compiling a detailed history of your symptoms and general health and will give you a thorough physical examination. Treatment is tailored to your individual condition and you will probably be taught specific exercises that you must undertake at home on a daily basis in between sessions. The physiotherapist will probably also give you detailed advice on posture, movement, lifting and carrying, as well as general lifestyle and exercise.

Physiotherapists use a variety of techniques depending on where they trained and their own personal preferences, but all fall into the following broad categories.

### Massage

Various forms of massage are used, both as therapy in their own right and as a warm-up procedure to relax mind and body and relieve pain before treatment such as mobilization. Various massage techniques may be used.

### Mobilization

Mobilization techniques are used to gradually increase the movement in stiff and painful joints in the spine and elsewhere. Gentle rhythmic movement is used to stretch the ligaments and move a joint or groups of joints near to the limits of their normal range. During mobilization you have a great deal of control and if the movement becomes painful, you can usually stop it by simply tensing your muscles.

Mobilization techniques are graded depending on how much force is exerted by the physiotherapist. The most forceful involves a deliberate thrust to push the joint or joints beyond the point at which movement stops in normal day-to-day activities. However, even in this technique the joint is never moved further than it can naturally go.

## Movement

Various exercises that you perform with the help of the physiotherapist and which are designed to strengthen muscles around joints are described as movement techniques. In some exercises, known as assisted movement, you work the muscles with the help of the physiotherapist and in others, known as resisted movement, the therapist pushes against you as you exercise.

Some simple exercises you can do at home are given on the pages 154–155.

## Traction

Traction can be as low-tech or high-tech as you like. At the do-it-yourself level, many people have found at least temporary relief from their back pain by hanging by their arms from the top of a door. At the other end of the scale there are various sorts of specialized equipment that you can use to apply traction while you lie horizontally or that allow you to hang upside down by your feet. Other equipment can apply traction specifically to the neck. The more advanced techniques should only be done under the supervision of your physiotherapist.

## Ultrasound

This is widely used by physiotherapists to treat injuries to muscles, tendons and ligaments. Ultrasound can relieve pain by reducing muscular spasm and areas of swelling. It uses ultra-high frequency sound waves, inaudible to the human ear,

which penetrate the skin harmlessly. The sound waves are emitted by a device that looks like a microphone and is passed slowly over your back. The procedure is completely painless.

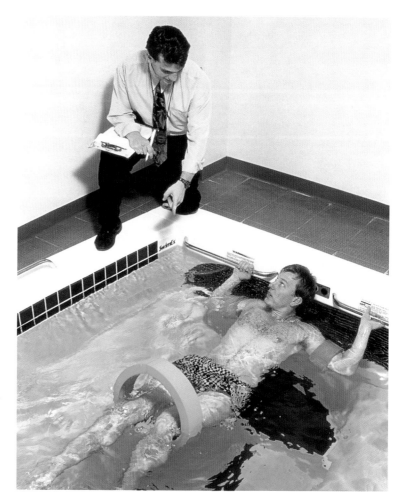

## Electrical therapy

Electrical devices can relieve back pain, but the benefits appear to be generally short-lived. The principle behind this therapy is that applying tiny amounts of electric current to areas around the pain site stimulates nerve endings in the skin and signals from these override the pain messages being sent to the brain. ▶

*Exercising in water can have excellent results for back-pain sufferers. Warm water eases pain and takes the weight off aching joints, making it easier to exercise.*

# Physiotherapy exercises

### Forward stretch

1 *Kneel on the floor, sitting back with your buttocks on your heels. Rest your hands on your knees and keep your back and neck straight. Breathe comfortably, into your abdomen.*

2 *Bend forward from your hips to put your hands on the floor with your arms straight. Then alternately round and flatten your back. Repeat as often as is comfortable.*

### Standing pelvic tilt

*Stand with your back to a wall. Holding your hands on your stomach so that you can feel the movement, flatten your lower back against the wall and relax. Repeat as often as is comfortable.*

### Lying pelvic tilt

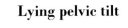

1 *Lie on you back, feet flat on the floor. Squeeze your buttocks and arch your lower back off the floor.*

2 *Hold the position for 1 to 2 seconds, then relax. Repeat a few times. Try to make the movement smooth and take it as far as is comfortable. Then allow your back to flatten on to the floor.*

# The cat

1 *Start on your hands and knees with your back straight, your hands directly below your shoulders and knees below your hips.*

**Find out more**

| | |
|---|---|
| *Stretching exercises* | 68 |
| *T'ai chi* | 96 |
| *Qigong* | 100 |

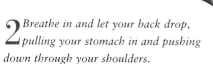

2 *Breathe in and let your back drop, pulling your stomach in and pushing down through your shoulders.*

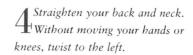

4 *Straighten your back and neck. Without moving your hands or knees, twist to the left.*

3 *Breathe out and push your back to curve upward. Drop your head down toward your chest.*

5 *Straighten your back and neck. Without moving your hands or knees, twist to the right. Repeat as often as is comfortable.*

---

# Press-ups

1 *Lie on your front with your forearms flat, your legs straight and your toes on the floor.*

2 *Gently raise your upper arms to push your body up and arch your back. Keep your legs and back relaxed. Repeat as often as is comfortable.*

# Drugs

*Several types, or classes, of drugs are commonly used to treat back pain. Some have to be prescribed by a doctor but many can be bought over the counter in any pharmacy and some are available in supermarkets.*

*In addition to pills and injections, you may find that externally applied products – such as a heat spray or gel, cold pack or hot or cold compresses – offer you relief from pain.*

The number of drugs on the market that can be used for back pain may, at first sight, appear bewildering but the majority are painkillers and fall into two distinct categories: analgesics, such as paracetamol, and non-steroidal anti-inflammatory drugs (NSAIDs), such as ibuprofen. Both types act as painkillers but work in different ways.

The use of drugs, and painkillers in particular, is one of the subjects that seems to polarize people. Some will put up with quite severe discomfort rather than "pollute" their body with anything resembling a drug. Others reach for the pill bottle at the first twinge of pain. As with most things, the most sensible path is probably somewhere in the middle.

If you are suffering serious back pain, don't be afraid to take a painkiller. Taken correctly for a short period of time, painkillers can reduce muscular spasm and help you cope during the acute phase of a bout of back pain. Healing is helped by a positive mental attitude and it is hard to be in this frame of mind if you are in constant, severe pain. Once the pain is under control, you are in a better frame of mind to start thinking about tackling its cause.

However, it is important not to treat yourself with painkillers as a substitute for seeking professional medical advice. You are in pain for a reason and it is important to find out what that reason is and to do something about it. Masking recurrent bouts of back trouble with painkillers is not solving the problem and you may well be courting greater problems in the long run if potentially serious conditions are ignored and left untreated.

## Side effects

The effectiveness of any drug has to be balanced against its unwanted side effects. All drugs have side effects, even those that are generally considered to be very safe and are easily bought in the local pharmacy or supermarket.

People vary greatly in their sensitivity to the side-effects of drugs. A drug that is perfectly tolerable for one person may make another feel unwell. As a general rule, the more powerful the drug and the longer you take it, the more likely you are to experience some of these unwanted side effects.

The side effects of the drugs most commonly used to treat back pain are summarized on pages 158–159.

## OTHERS DRUGS FOR BACK PAIN

Two other types of drug are sometimes used to treat back pain: muscle relaxants and antidepressants. Both types of drugs have to be prescribed by a doctor.

### Muscle relaxants

These are believed to relieve back pain by relaxing the painful muscle spasm that often follows back injury. Because these drugs have their effect in the brain, they can make you sleepy and impair your concentration. So if you have to drive or operate machinery they may not be suitable for you.

The muscle relaxants should only be taken for a short period of time – not more than two weeks at the most. Once the muscle spasm has eased you should stop taking them, as with some drugs of this type, particularly tranquillizers, there is a risk of addiction.

### Antidepressants

It may seem a bit odd to take an antidepressant drug when you have a physical problem like back pain. But research shows that antidepressants can be an effective treatment for long-term or chronic pain. There is a close link between chronic pain and depression in that depression can manifest itself in the form of pain and long-term pain can cause depression. ▶

*The most commonly used drugs for back pain are analgesics, NSAIDs, muscle relaxants and antidepressants.*

## CHEMONUCLEOLYSIS OR DISCOLYSIS

*A chemical alternative to surgery for a prolapsed disc involves an injection in a process known as chemonucleolysis or discolysis. The drug used is a substance called chymopapain from the tropical papaya or pawpaw. In the hot countries where it grows naturally the papaya is renowned as an aid to digestion.*

*When chymopapain is injected into the prolapsed disc it dissolves part of it. As a result, the disc shrinks and stops pressing on sensitive structures, such as nearby nerve roots. Doctors give the injection under local anaesthetic and X-rays ensure the chymopapain is injected into exactly the right spot.*

*The procedure can give dramatic relief from problems such as severe sciatica and, while not risk-free, has less risk of complications than surgery.*

# Drugs

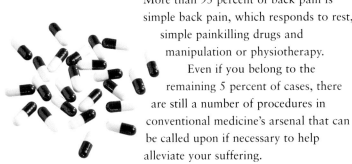

▸ **MORE SERIOUS BACK PAIN**

More than 95 percent of back pain is simple back pain, which responds to rest, simple painkilling drugs and manipulation or physiotherapy.

Even if you belong to the remaining 5 percent of cases, there are still a number of procedures in conventional medicine's arsenal that can be called upon if necessary to help alleviate your suffering.

## Injections

If your pain is not eased by any of the normally prescribed medications, pain-relieving drugs can be injected directly into the affected area of the back. Normally doctors use a corticosteroid – which alleviates pain by reducing inflammation and swelling – mixed with a local anaesthetic. These injections are unpleasant but they can give welcome relief from severe pain.

## DRUGS USED TO TREAT BACK PAIN

| | |
|---|---|
| SIMPLE PAINKILLERS | Examples are aspirin (also a non-steroidal anti-inflammatory drug or NSAID) and paracetamol. Used for mild to moderate pain. There are few side effects but aspirin can irritate the lining of the stomach and should not be taken if you have a history of stomach or duodenal ulcers. Paracetamol is highly poisonous to the liver in overdose. Available over the counter. |
| COMPOUND ANALGESICS | A combination of a painkiller and an opiate. In Australia and New Zealand, examples are paracetamol with codeine or dextropropoxyphene hydrochloride, and aspirin with codeine (some available only on prescription); in South Africa, paracetamol with dextropropoxyphene and aspirin with codeine. Used for mild to moderate pain. Side effects include drowsiness and constipation. |
| NARCOTIC OR OPIOID ANALGESICS | "Narcotic" comes from the Greek *narkos*, meaning "to numb". These powerful drugs contain opiates such as morphine, codeine, pethidine and methadone. Used for severe pain that does not respond to simple painkillers and compound analgesics (see above) or NSAIDs (see below). Side effects include drowsiness and constipation. They are effective painkillers but carry a risk of addiction and should only be used for short periods. Only available on prescription from your doctor. |
| NON-STEROIDAL ANTI-INFLAMMATORY DRUGS (NSAIDs) | The most commonly used drugs for back pain, believed to work by reducing local inflammation and swelling. Examples of NSAIDs used in Australia and New Zealand include ibuprofen, naproxen, piroxicam and diclofenac; in South Africa, ibuprofen and mefenamic acid. Used for mild to moderate pain. Side effects include indigestion, stomach upsets and, occasionally, ulcers. Available over the counter or on doctor's prescription, depending on the strength and type of preparation. |

If you have severe pain caused by a problem such as a prolapsed disc that is not responding to other treatment or medication, a similar mixture of drugs can be injected directly into the spinal canal near the base of the spine. This is known as an epidural.

An epidural blocks the pain signals travelling between the site of pain and the brain, numbing the area around the prolapse; it also reduces inflammation.

This is a safe, but highly skilled procedure that is normally only carried out in hospital by an experienced anaesthetist. However, many back-pain sufferers have found that an epidural has given them several weeks' relief from pain.

Side effects are rare, although some people have suffered from nausea, dizziness or headaches following an epidural. These effects are temporary and can be controlled with other drugs.

**Find out more**

| | |
|---|---|
| *Prolapsed disc* | *43* |
| *Muscular problems* | *50* |
| *Sudden pain* | *76* |

## DRUGS USED TO TREAT BACK PAIN

| | |
|---|---|
| MUSCLE RELAXANTS | These drugs make you sleepy and relaxed and therefore reduce the muscle spasms that can cause pain. Examples include orphenadrine citrate (orphenadrine in South Africa) and tranquillizers such as diazepam. Used for mild to moderate pain. Side effects include drowsiness, headaches, dizziness and blurred vision. Available on prescription from your doctor. |
| ANTIDEPRESSANTS | Used to treat conditions involving long-term or chronic pain. Depression can manifest itself as chronic pain and the pain brings depression. If the depression is lifted, pain becomes less troublesome. There are many different antidepressants but most fall into one of two categories: selective serotonin reuptake inhibitors (SSRIs) and tricyclic antidepressants. The latter are effective but have a high level of side effects, including dry mouth, drowsiness, blurred vision, dizziness and weight gain. The SSRIs, which are newer drugs, are just as effective but have fewer serious side effects. |
| INJECTED DRUGS | These are used for severe pain, such as a damaged facet joint, a trigger point or a prolapsed disc pressing on a nerve root that will not respond to any of the above medications. A mixture of a corticosteroid – a hormone with powerful anti-inflammatory effects – and a local anaesthetic is normally injected directly into a facet joint or trigger point or, in the case of a prolapsed disc, into the spinal canal – a procedure known as an epidural. Side effects are rare. |
| CHEMONUCLEOLYSIS OR DISCOLYSIS | A chemical alternative to surgery for a prolapsed disc. A substance, known as chymopapain, is injected into the prolapsed disc and dissolves its nucleus. The disc shrinks, relieving pressure on sensitive structures nearby. Side effects include a sore back for several weeks. Some people can suffer an allergic reaction to chymopapain but drugs are usually given beforehand to prevent this. |

# Surgery to correct back problems

*Surgery is a last resort in the conventional treatment of back pain. It will only be considered if all other forms of treatment have failed. The results of surgery can never be guaranteed.*

Surgery today is very safe. Nevertheless, there are certain risks associated with any operation, including the possibility of an adverse reaction to the anaesthetic, the risk of a blood clot lodging in the lungs or the brain, an increased risk of chest infection and haemorrhage – sudden blood loss, which occasionally requires a blood transfusion.

In addition, with back surgery there is always the possibility of damage to the spinal cord, which can result in paralysis. The chances of any of these complications occurring are remote. For example, the chance of damage to the spinal cord and nerves as a result of a spinal operation is about one in 5,000. But the risks must be weighed in the balance when a decision is made to refer anyone for surgery.

Fears about an operation should be talked through with your doctor and the surgeon. You should not feel pressurized and should only agree to go ahead with the operation if you feel satisfied that the potential benefits significantly outweigh the risks. A sympathetic doctor will support you in your cautious approach.

No surgeon, however skilled, can guarantee that an operation will be successful and it is important to have realistic expectations of the outcome. The back is a complex structure and by the time you eventually undergo surgery, the original problem may have thrown other areas out of balance and caused them to become strained and painful in their turn.

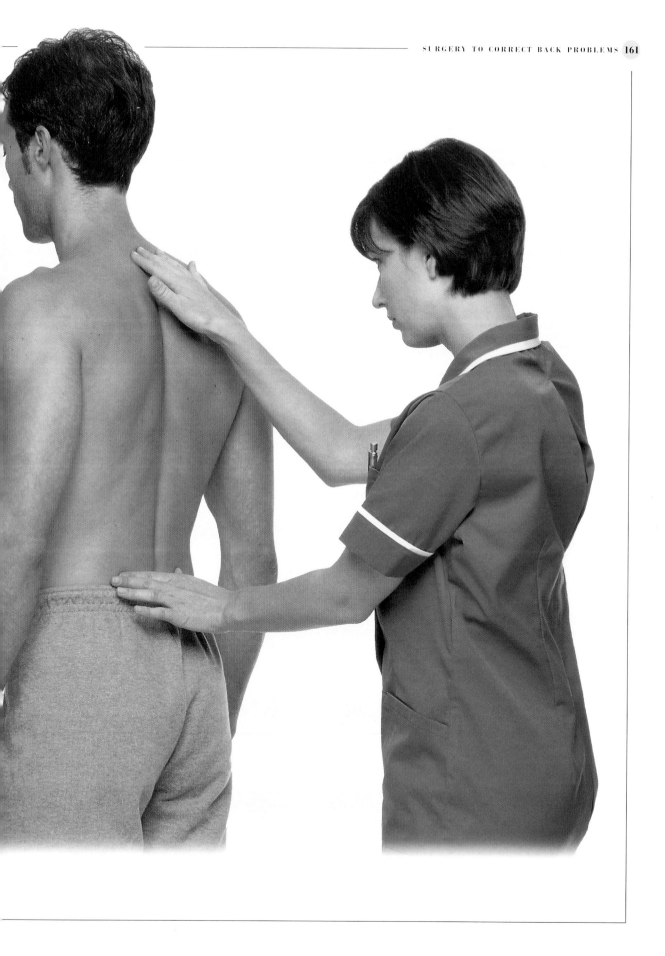

# The most common back operations

*Generally, surgery is more successful in curing problems arising from a single structural injury than in relieving back pain that results from years of gradual deterioration. By far the most common reason for back surgery is to treat prolapsed discs.*

You are likely to be chosen for surgery only for a specific reason. This may be severe, continuous pain caused by a prolapsed disc pressing on a nerve, or evidence of spinal stenosis where the spinal canal has become narrowed, perhaps by osteophytes (bony growths on the vertebrae) compressing the spinal cord. Occasionally, surgery is the only option and needs to be carried out quickly. This sort of emergency can occur if the *cauda equina* becomes compressed by a large disc prolapse, for example.

In a normal situation, as a possible candidate for surgery you will have to undergo various investigations so that the surgeon can build up as detailed a picture as possible about your condition before deciding if surgery is an option. For

example, the location of a disc prolapse can be ascertained by a physical examination; however, the exact extent of the problem can only be discovered by taking sophisticated tests such as myelography or a CT or MRI scan.

If these tests show that an operation can be carried out, the surgeon will discuss the situation with you, explaining the advantages and disadvantages of surgery, its chances of success and the amount of improvement you can expect. If, after this, you are still unsure about whether you wish to go ahead, you are perfectly free to refuse to have the operation. If you do undergo surgery and your condition does not improve, be wary of agreeing to a second operation as research suggests that the chances of success are much lower for repeat procedures of this kind.

One important, non-medical factor that needs to be considered in your decision about surgery is how you will cope when you are discharged from hospital after the operation. The chances are that you will be unable to carry out normal daily tasks, such as cooking, cleaning and shopping, for several weeks. If you do not have a partner or family members who can help, you may have to consider the expensive options of a booking into a convalescent home or paying for someone to come in and look after you.

The procedures described on the following pages are among the most common operations for back problems.

## SPINAL SURGERY: A NEW PROCEDURE

*One of the most radical spinal operations ever undertaken was carried out by surgeons at Bristol, England, in the late 1990s. The patient was a 36-year-old woman suffering from ankylosing spondylitis, which had caused the vertebrae in her neck to fuse. She subsequently broke her neck in a fall and when the injury healed, her head was fixed facing downward and to the right.*

*In a 17-hour operation surgeons made an incision into the back of her neck to expose the spine. They then detached her head from her spine so that it was attached only by the spinal cord, blood vessels and tissues. A wedge was cut into the base of the skull and into the top vertebra. The skull was then placed in a normal, forward-looking position and re-attached to the spine using a metal plate and screws. The operation was a success and the woman recovered fully.*

## Discectomy

Sometimes a prolapsed disc remains pressing on a nerve, causing sciatica if the problem is in the lower back or brachialgia if it is higher up. In this situation a discectomy may be carried out to remove the part of the disc that is protruding and compressing the nerve.

The surgeon makes an incision to expose the ligaments that cover the spine. He or she then carefully cuts through the ligaments to expose the nerves and the vertebrae. The surgeon locates the prolapsed disc and removes the protruding part, leaving the main body of the disc intact. He or she then checks to see if the newly freed nerve is able to move easily. If the nerve is impeded in any way, the surgeon will remove tiny pieces of bone from the vertebrae to ease its passage. The ligaments, muscle and skin are then stitched back together.

Today, an increasing number of these operations are carried out using microsurgery. This involves making a small incision, perhaps no more than 2.5 cm (1 in) long, and operating through this using a telescopic viewing tube and specially designed surgical instruments.

The advantage of this technique is that there is less disruption and damage to the muscles, ligaments and other tissues and, as a result, recovery is generally quicker.

Discectomy can result in dramatic relief from back pain. Following the operation you will probably be encouraged to get up and move about after a couple of days, although you may have to wear a corset to support your back for a couple of weeks. Most people recover well from the operation and can return to work within a few months.

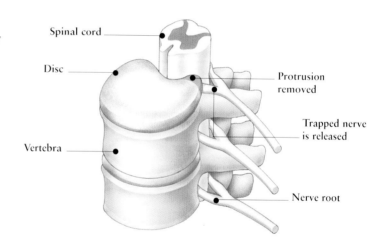

Spinal cord — Disc — Vertebra — Protrusion removed — Trapped nerve is released — Nerve root

## Decompression

As with discectomy, this operation is carried out to relieve pressure on a nerve or on the spinal cord itself. However, in this case the pressure is not exerted by a prolapsed disc but by problems connected with the bones of the spine.

The operation may be needed in cases of spondylolisthesis, when a vertebral arch breaks in two causing the vertebra to slip out of line and press on a nerve root or on the spinal cord. This can result in severe pain. ▶

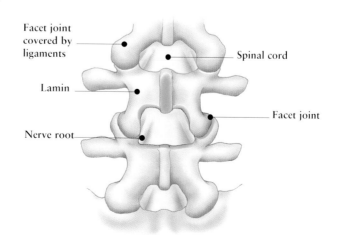

Facet joint covered by ligaments — Lamin — Nerve root — Spinal cord — Facet joint

# The most common back operations

▶ Alternatively, nerves or the spinal cord can be compressed by osteophytes growing into the gaps between the vertebrae or into the spinal canal.

The surgeon makes an incision and carefully removes pieces of bone to relieve the pressure on the nerve roots or the spinal cord.

Recovery from decompression is normally straightforward and you should be able to return to normal activities, including work, within a few months.

## Spinal fusion

This procedure is used to stabilize and stiffen the spine. It may be necessary if any facet joints are diseased and frequently slip out of alignment, or to prevent problems such as spondylolisthesis from increasing. It can also be used to stabilize the lower spine if parts of it move too much when you bend over. This problem, known as lumbar instability, can result in back pain and frequent bouts of sciatica. Spinal fusion is only used when there is no other choice, since the section of the spine fused in this way remains permanently rigid and unbending.

The operation normally involves taking strips of bone from another part of the body, usually the hips or pelvis, and grafting them vertically across two or three vertebrae. Alternatively, one or more discs are removed and the empty space packed with tiny pieces of bone, which fuse with the vertebrae above and below, locking that part of the spine rigid. Taking bone from the hips or pelvis has no lasting ill-effects but the area will be painful for quite a while.

Spinal fusion is much more serious than discectomy or decompression and in the past you would have had to lie in bed encased in plaster for a month and then stay in bed for perhaps another two or three months. Today, you will probably be allowed out of bed after a couple of weeks but you will probably have to wear a corset for a month or so. Spinal fusion leaves the back greatly weakened and it can take up to a year to recover fully. It is important to begin working with a physiotherapist as soon as you are fit enough in order to regain as much strength and flexibility as possible.

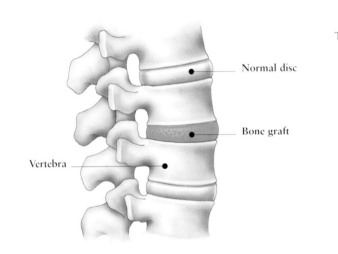

Normal disc

Bone graft

Vertebra

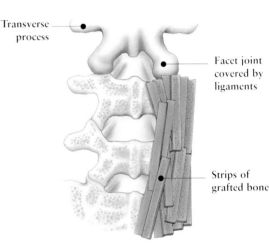

Transverse process

Facet joint covered by ligaments

Strips of grafted bone

## Neck surgery

Surgeons are more reluctant to operate on the neck than on any other part of the spine since, if anything goes wrong, there is a risk of paralysis in all four limbs.

If a prolapsed disc is pressing on the spinal cord or vertebrae in your neck have become unstable, perhaps due to diseased facet joints, surgery may be necessary. One of the most common forms of neck surgery is a fusion operation.

The surgeon operates through an incision in the front of the neck and removes an entire disc. The discs in the neck are smaller than those elsewhere in the spine and, as the resulting gap is narrower, the vertebrae fuse together without the need of bone grafts.

Fusion operations in the neck require a stay of only a few days in hospital. You will have to wear a support collar for a few months while the vertebrae fuse.

## Surgery to straighten the spine

Sometimes surgery is necessary for scoliosis – curvature of the spine. In the vast majority of cases of scoliosis the curve is so slight that no treatment is required but in severe cases, such as when the condition begins in childhood, action is often needed to prevent the condition worsening and causing serious deformity.

There are several surgical methods used to treat this sort of scoliosis. The most common technique uses a telescopic metal rod, known as a Harrington rod. The surgeon makes an incision through the skin, muscle and ligaments and exposes the spine along the whole length of the curve. The Harrington rod is then positioned and fixed along the concave side of the spine and telescoped out to straighten the curve. Pieces of bone taken from the hips or pelvis are then grafted across the vertebrae of the curved section to lock it straight and rigid.

Another method involves removing the vertebral discs in the curved part of the spine. Holes are then drilled through the vertebrae. Bolts are slotted through these holes and attached to a steel cable which runs down the convex side of the curving spine. The cable is then tightened up, pulling the spine straight.

Although surgical procedures for scoliosis result in a very rigid back, they are usually successful at preventing serious deformity as a child suffering from this condition grows up.

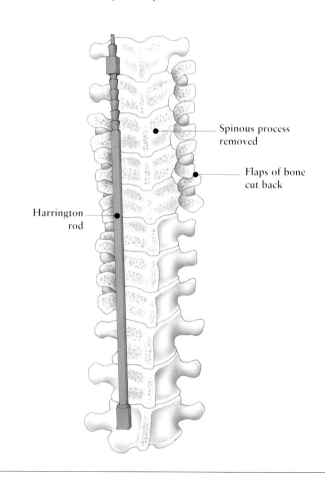

Spinous process removed

Flaps of bone cut back

Harrington rod

# After back surgery

*There are a number of things you can do after an operation to become fit for normal life again. Post-operation treatment, from an occupational therapist or sports injuries therapist, can be as important as the operation itself.*

Immediately after your operation, you will be taken from the operating theatre to a recovery room or high-level care unit, where you will stay until the doctors feel your condition is stable. You will then be taken back to your ward on a trolley. You will be given painkillers to help relieve pain after the operation. Doctors and nurses will be keen to get you walking as soon as possible, since it is now well known that moderate exercise speeds healing and improves health.

Even after a successful operation, your back is unlikely to be as good as new. The muscles of your back will be weakened by the operation and convalescence and will need to be strengthened. Meanwhile, the secondary problems will still be there and will need to be tackled, perhaps with other forms of therapy.

To a certain extent the recovery process depends on you. The surgery can only be successful if you have the determination to do your part and are prepared to make the effort to recover your strength and fitness. This may include a lengthy course of physiotherapy and perhaps attending a "back school" if there is one in a hospital nearby.

## Rehabilitation centres

Normally run by physiotherapists, occupational therapists or sports therapists, under the supervision of doctors, rehabilitation centres specialize in trying to return you to full fitness after your operation. They concentrate on teaching you how to work with any aids you may have been fitted with, such as a corset or a collar, and toning up your muscles to cope.

## Support for your back

The subject of support corsets and collars for back pain is controversial. Advocates maintain that sometimes a painful back or neck needs extra support. They argue that if you are recovering from a back operation, for example, and have to return to work, wearing a corset for a week or so can help you to do so without increasing the risk of a relapse. Or if you have suffered a whiplash-type injury, a neck collar can help support the weight of your head while the inflammation around the spinal joints and ligaments subsides and healing begins.

Medical opinion is divided about the

*A collar can provide neck support after an operation. Your physiotherapist will make sure that it is appropriate in your case.*

*Surgery can help you return to a full and active life. Taking time to relax and enjoy yourself is an important part of the recovery process.*

advantages and disadvantages of these kinds of supports. Research results are conflicting, with some studies showing that there can be some benefit and others finding no advantage whatsoever.

Most experts do agree, however, that if you try wearing a corset or collar and you find it helps, you should wear it for as short a period of time as possible since it is all too easy to become dependent upon it. Wearing a corset or collar for more than a few weeks can actually do more harm than good because unused muscles may weaken and the spinal joints become stiff in a surprisingly short period.

Corsets for back pain come in all shapes and sizes. Some just cover the lumbar region while others encase you from the lower ribs to the buttocks. They are thought to work in two ways. They increase the pressure in your abdomen and reduce the strain in your lower back,

and they restrict your movements. This has the effect of reducing pain and forces you to keep your back straight and to bend your knees while lifting and carrying out other daily activities.

Collars are believed to support the weight of your head and take pressure off the vertebrae in your neck. Corsets and collars also keep your back or neck warm and this, combined with the support they provide, can help muscles that are tense or in spasm relax, easing pain.

Corsets and collars can be bought in shops specializing in equipment for back pain or by mail order and are also often available through the health services and, particularly, via physiotherapy clinics. If you are going to use a corset or collar it is important that it is the right one for you and that it fits correctly – take advice from your doctor or from a physiotherapist before buying one.

# Glossary

**Acupuncture points** – specific points along the meridians at which the flow of *qi* or *chi*, the life energy of the universe, can be stimulated.

**Acute** – occurring suddenly and painfully; of short duration (compare chronic).

**Analgesic** – a pain-relieving substance or drug.

**Ankylosing spondylitis** – a form of arthritis in which the joints of the spine gradually stiffen and can lock rigid.

**Avulsion** – a fracture in which the tip of a bony process, one of the protrusions at the rear of the vertebrae, is cracked or pulled off.

**Brachialgia** – pain in the arm and/or hand that may be caused by compression of a nerve. It may be accompanied by numbness or pins and needles and muscle weakness.

**Cartilage** – the tough and slippery covering at the end of bones where they meet to form joints.

**Cauda equina** – the sheaf of nerves that fan out from the bottom of the spinal cord.

**Cervical spine** – the part of the spine that forms the neck.

**Chi** – another spelling of qi, the universal life-energy in Traditional Chinese Medicine.

**Chronic** – of long-term duration.

**Compression** – pressure on a nerve or the spinal cord, perhaps by a prolapsed disc.

**Crush fracture** – the collapse of a vertebra.

**Disc, intervertebral** – a fibrous shock-absorbing pad that sits between the individual vertebrae.

**Dural sleeves** – the sheaths encasing and protecting the nerve roots as they branch off from the spinal cord.

**Dural tube** – the sheath of the spinal cord, which consists of three membranes – the meninges – one inside the other.

**Epidural** – an injection of pain-killing drugs into the spinal canal in the lower back.

**Essential oil** – an aromatic liquid, extracted from a plant, which aromatherapists believe contains the life-force of the plant.

**Facet joint** – one of the chain of small joints that link the bony processes at the rear of the vertebrae to each other.

**Ligament** – a band of tough, fibrous tissue that supports bones at a joint and controls the way in which they can move.

**Lumbago** – pain in the lower back.

**Lumbar** – relating to the lower part of the spine, from the waist to the hips.

**Meridian** – a channel that runs through the body carrying the life-force, *qi* or *chi*. There are 14 main meridians.

**Microfracture** – a tiny fracture in the flat, weight-bearing surface of a vertebra where it joins the disc or in one of the transverse processes, the bony protrusions at the back of the vertebrae.

**Osteophytes** – bony, spurlike growths on or around the vertebrae. Osteophytes are a feature of osteoarthritis.

**Osteoporosis** – a condition in which bones become thin and brittle, normally associated with ageing.

**Prana** – the fundamental life energy of the universe in Ayurvedic medicine, the traditional Indian system of healing. Also known as *qi* or *chi* in Traditional Chinese Medicine.

**Process, bony or transverse** – one of three protrusions at the rear of each vertebra, which join the vertebrae together, at the facet joints.

**Prolapsed disc** – the rupture of a disc's outer casing and the leakage of part of its nucleus.

**Qi** (pronounced "chee") – in Traditional Chinese Medicine, the fundamental life energy of the universe, also known as *chi*; the equivalent of *prana* in Ayurvedic medicine.

**Sacroiliac joints** – the two joints that join the bottom of the spine to the pelvis.

**Sciatica** – pain in a buttock and down one leg. It may be accompanied by numbness or pins and needles. Sciatica can be caused by the compression of a sciatic nerve, perhaps by a prolapsed disc.

**Scoliosis** – sideways curvature of the spine.

**Spondylolisthesis** – a condition of the spine in which the vertebral arch breaks right through and the vertebra slips out of line. It is often a progression of spondylolysis.

**Spondylolysis** – a fracture in the vertebral arch in the lower lumbar spine.

**Spinal canal** – the bony channel formed from the neural arch through which the spinal cord runs.

**Spinal stenosis** – a narrowing of the spinal canal, through which the spinal cord passes, perhaps by a prolapsed disc or by the growth of osteophytes.

**Succussion** – the process by which a homeopathic remedy is made more powerful or potentized. Each time the remedy is diluted it is shaken to imprint the energy of the original substance on molecules in the liquid.

**Synovial fluid** – a fluid that lubricates the joints.

**Tendon** – a tough band of tissue connecting muscle to bone.

**Thoracic spine** – the part of the spine from the neck to the waist.

**Tincture** – a herbal remedy prepared by chopping or grinding up a plant and soaking it in an alcohol solution. The mixture is left to stand for several weeks, then the liquid is strained off and taken by mouth.

**Tisane** – an infusion of a herbal remedy prepared in a way similar to brewing tea. The herbs are infused in hot water in a teapot for about 10 minutes, the liquid is poured off and drunk hot or cold.

**Vertebra** (plural vertebrae) – one of the individual bones of the spine.

**Vertebral, or neural arch** – a bony arch at the rear of each vertebra. The arches of all the vertebrae together form the spinal canal through which the spinal cord runs.

**Whiplash injury** – a strain or tear injury to the ligaments supporting the bones of the neck. It usually occurs when the head is thrown violently backward and forward as in a car crash.

**Wry neck** – pain and restricted movement in the neck that may be the result of a facet joint or disc problem.

# Useful Organizations

**Back Care (Registered as the National Back Pain Association)**
16 Elmtree Road
Teddington
Middlesex
TW11 8ST
Tel: 020 8977 5474

## ACUPUNTURE
**Acupuncture Association of Chartered Physiotherapists**
www.aacp.uk.com

**British Acupuncture Council:**
**The British Acupuncture Council (BAcC)**
63 Jeddo Road
London W12 9HQ
Tel: 020 8735 0400

**British Medical Acupuncture Society**
BMAS House
3 Winnington Court
Northwich
Cheshire CW8 1AQ
Tel: 01606 786782

## ALEXANDER TECHNIQUE
**Society of Teachers of the Alexander Technique**
1st Floor, Linton House
39– 1 Highgate Road
London NW5 1RS
Tel: 0845 230 7828

## CHINESE MEDICINE
**Institue of Chinese Medicine**
44 Chandos Place
London WC2
Tel: 020 7836 5220

## COMPLEMENTARY MEDICINE
**Institute for Complementary Medicine**
PO Box 194
London SE16 7QZ
Tel: 020 7237 5165

**Research Council for Complementary Medicine**
www.rccm.org.uk

**British Complementary Medicine Association**
PO Box 5122
Bournemouth BH8 0WG
Tel: 0845 345 5977

**British Holistic Medical Association**
PO Box 371
Bridgwater
Somerset TA6 9BG
Tel: 01278 722 000

## HERBALISM
**National Institute of Medical Herbalists**
Elm House
54 Mary Arches Street
Exeter EX4 3BA
Tel: 01392 426022

## HOMEOPATHY
**British Homeopathic Association**
Hahnemann House
29 Park Street West
Luton LU1 3BE
Tel: 0870 444 3950

## HYPNOSIS
**British Society for Medical and Dental Hypnosis:**
National Office:
28 Dale Park Gardens
Cookridge
Leeds LS16 7PT
Tel: 07000 560309

## MANIPULATION THERAPIES
**British Chiropractic Association**
59 Castle Street
Reading
Berkshire RG1 7SN
Tel: 0118 950 5950

**British Osteopathic Association**
Langham House West
Mill Street
Luton
Bedfordshire LU1 2NA
Tel: 01582 488455

**Chartered Society of Physiotherapy**
14 Bedford Row
London WC1 4ED
Tel: 020 7306 6666

**The Feldenkrais Guild**
Tel: 07000 785 506
www.feldenkrais.co.uk

## PSYCHOTHERAPY AND COUNSELLING
**British Association for Counselling**
BACP House
35 – 37 Albert Street
Rugby
Warwickshire CV21 2SG

**British Association of Psychotherapists**
37 Mapesbury Road
London NW2 4HJ
Tel: 020 8452 9823

## REFLEXOLOGY
**British Reflexology Association**
Monks Orchard
Whitbourne
Worcestershire WR6 5RB
Tel: 01886 21207

## YOGA
**Yoga Biomedical Trust**
90 -92 Pentonville Road,
London N1 9HS,
Tel: 020 7689 3040

# Index

# Acknowledgments

The publishers wish to acknowledge the invaluable contribution made to this book by Andrew Sydenham who took all the photographs except:

Cover and page 3 Tony Latham; 4 Science Photo Library; 10 Tony Latham; 15 (left) Science Photo Library; 18 Science Photo Library; 20 Tony Stone Images; 37 (top) Rex Features; 38 Tony Latham; 42 Laura Wickenden; 43 Science Photo Library; 45 (left) Science Photo Library; 50 (left) Science Photo Library; (right) The Stock Market; 52 Allsport/Chris Cole; 53 Laura Wickenden; 55 Science Photo Library; 57 Science Photo Library; 59 (right) Science Photo Library; 62 The Stock Market; 64 The Stock Market; 65 (top) Camera Press; 66 Camera Press; 67 The Stock Market; 74 Tony Stone Images; 81 Science Photo Library; 84 Laura Wickenden; 92 Science Photo Library;

94 The Stock Market; 97 E. T. Archive; 102 Camera Press; 103 James Holmes/Science Photo Library; 105 Images Colour Library; 108 Science Photo Library; 109 Science Photo Library; 110 (top) Science Photo Library; (bottom) Laura Wickenden; 111 Paul Biddle & Tim Malyon/Science Photo Library; 112 Rex Features; 113 Laura Wickenden; 114 Science Photo Library; 118 Laura Wickenden; 119 The Stock Market; 120 Science Photo Library; 121 Science Photo Library; 125 Science Photo Library; 127 Science Photo Library; 130 The Hutchison Library; 132 E. T. Archive; 138 The Freud Museum; 140 (top) John Walmsley; 142 (top) Jo Foord; (bottom) Laura Wickenden; 143 Panos Pictures; 144 Science Photo Library; 146 The Stock Market; 149 Henry Arden; 150 Science Photo Library; 151 Science Photo Library; 153 Science Photo Library; 157 Science Photo Library; 161 Henry Arden; 166 The Stock Market; 167 Image Bank.